Music Room

Namita Devidayal

RANDOM HOUSE INDIA

Published by Random House India in 2008

Fifth impression in 2012

Copyright © Namita Devidayal 2007

Random House Publishers India Private Limited
Windsor IT Park, 7th Floor, Tower-B,
A-1, Sector-125, Noida-201301, UP

Random House Group Limited
20 Vauxhall Bridge Road
London SW1V 2SA
United Kingdom

ISBN 978 81 8400 054 2

Typeset by Weserve Universe and Bukprint
Printed and bound in India by Replika Press Private Limited

For sale in the Indian subcontinent only

To baiji, with love

Contents

Prologue
Bhairavi

A raga should be performed such that, within a few minutes, both the performer and the audience should be able to see it standing in front of them...

Vilayat Khan, sitar player

It was a little before five. Dhondutai shivered as a breeze wafted in through the window. She lay in bed for a few minutes, mouthing a silent prayer, and flexed her stiff, aching leg. She tried to slip back into sleep so she could resume her favorite dream of sitting on a swing near the goddess temple by the river. When the rooster crowed a second time, she roused herself and shuffled towards the bathroom.

Dhondutai walked into the music room and picked up the tanpura, wincing slightly at the pain in her leg as she sat down to tune it. She ran her fingers over its taut strings and adjusted the ivory beads at the end, where the instrument's slender stem ballooned into a gleaming gourd. When the pitch was perfect, she began to strum the four strings in a regular motion. The notes swirled into the air around her and she forgot her pain, the cold room, the milkman who always delivered late, and melted into the timeless drone.

She started with the lower notes, chanting them one at a time like in a guttural prayer. Then, gradually, as a sliver of morning light slipped into the room, illuminating a square on the faded paisley-patterned carpet, she started moving higher up the scale. She was singing Bhairavi, an early morning raga filled with plaintive half notes.

Bhairavi is the wife of the cosmic dancer-destroyer Shiva. The raga is moody, like the mythical goddess. She is sometimes a pining lover, at other times a devotee,

3

sometimes a seductress and, always, the mysterious female force which overpowers evil.

Dhondutai sang with her eyes closed, touching each note with tenderness, as if she was slowly wrapping herself into a great cocoon of sound. Sensing an unnatural source of light, her eyes opened, but she continued to sing while her vision followed the trail of light to the corner of the room. As she reached the raga's highest and most sublime note, she heard a sigh of pleasure and the goddess appeared before her, smiling. Startled, Dhondutai shut her eyes, and when she opened them, the vision was gone.

She put down her tanpura and went to the door to pick up her milk bottle. Her day had begun well.

Part I
Kennedy Bridge

One

I was dragged into the world of music as a reluctant ten-year-old. One summer evening, while my friends went off to swim at the Willingdon Club, my mother packed me into a car and said we were going to meet a music teacher.

The music teacher lived in an old building under Kennedy Bridge, ten minutes away from the tree-lined streets of Cumballa Hill where we lived. Kennedy Bridge was a neighbourhood known for prostitutes and gentlemen's clubs, but not for musicians. The only other time I had heard of Kennedy Bridge was when my parents joked about their adventurous evening in a mujrah dance parlor many years ago. They recalled the night vividly—the pimp with a red kerchief around his neck who negotiated with them on the curbside under the bridge; the walk up to room number 88 on the second floor of a building which smelled of urine; the green windows which shielded its inhabitants from any prying eyes on the bridge that heaved with traffic just a few feet away; and a woman called Chandni, draped in a sequined nylon sari, who gyrated under faux chandeliers and leaned forward so far under my father's nose that he bursts into giggles every time he describes the moment.

But, like in most neighbourhoods in Bombay, daylight masked what went on after hours. During the day, the area under Kennedy Bridge was like any other crowded street, throbbing with people hawking their wares or hurrying along. Across the street from the whore houses stood an old stone convent called Queen Mary School. Next to it was a row of auto parts stores. And, at the end of the road, deep inside a residential colony called Congress House, lived a great musician.

It was five in the evening when my mother and I got there. We parked along the curb and walked past the storefronts displaying lubes and spanners to get to the grey disconsolate building. There was no lift, so we trudged up the stairs to a tiny apartment on the third floor. A family of three lived on one side of the kitchen. The music teacher lived on the other side as a paying guest, in a room with pale, pistachio-colored walls. Her solitary companion in this room was her mother, whom she called Ayi.

My teacher-to-be was waiting for us with a cherubic smile. She was about five feet tall and was clad in a white sari, starched crisp. Her black hair was liberally oiled. I was delighted to note that her tiny bun was a ponytail in disguise. She was remarkably youthful for a fifty-year-old which, I later learned, she firmly attributed to never having married.

Sequestered in her tiny apartment, with her two gleaming tanpuras that stood against the wall, she seemed oblivious to the men who loitered below her window next to the brothels, spitting betel juice on the filthy walls of the buildings that housed their fantasies. It was like wading through a dirty pond to get to a beautiful lotus in the center.

The walls of her room were bare except for three portraits. There was a technicolor Ganesh, torn off an old pharmaceutical company calendar. Next to it, a portrait of her teacher, the legendary Kesarbai Kerkar; head covered with a white sari, hair parted on the side, and a string of pearls around her neck. On the adjoining wall was a faded sepia photograph of Dhondutai's parents soon after they were married—her father, a stiff Brahmin in a coat and dhoti, sitting upright with his knees apart, and her mother, a frail, beautiful woman in a nine-yard sari pulled tightly around her shoulders, sitting pigeon-toed, her feet pointing towards each other, acutely self-conscious.

My attention was drawn to a dollhouse-like altar, tucked away in a corner of the room. Inside, was the entire cast of the Hindu pantheon—tiny silver and brass idols of baby Krishna, Ganesh, Saraswati, Laxmi, a couple of silver coins, and a picture of an almost naked holy man sitting in meditation. The gods had been polished and decorated with a touch of kumkum. In front of each lay a sprinkling of fresh jasmine flowers whose fragrance lingered faintly. On top of the temple flickered an orange bulb, fashioned to simulate a live flame. It instantly amused me.

As I learnt later, the room was a semblance of another home—her ancestral bungalow in Kolhapur, the town she had left behind, where temple chimes wafted in with the evening breeze and jasmine grew in abundance. This is the kind of compromise Bombay forces on those who come to her, the price they must pay for her pleasures.

'Say namaste to her,' my mother nudged me.

'She can call me baiji.' Dhondutai beamed.

'Baap re, she is quite tall for her age,' Dhondutai continued, holding my chin, and peering down at my face affectionately.

9

'Yes, both of us are tall. Hopefully, art runs in the family too,' my mother joked, as usual getting straight to the point.

'She's still quite young. Let's start with twice a week—Tuesday and Thursday? From five to six? That will give her enough time to freshen up when she gets back from school. Then, depending on how she progresses, we'll firm up the days.'

While my fate was being decided, I was intrigued by an old bald lady with a few wisps of grey hair pulled into a tiny bun, who was pouting at the visitors from a corner of the room. It was Dhondutai's mother, Ayi, a wizened vestige of the woman in the photograph. She must have been at least eighty. I grinned at her and got a lovely, toothless smile in return.

As I was leaving the room, my eyes wandered once more to the shrine with the flickering lamp. Catching my gaze, Dhondutai laughed and beckoned to me to come closer for a peek. I sat in front of the gods awkwardly, conscious of her behind me, of my mother hovering impatiently at the door, of Ayi staring into space, and of the strange new room that was going to be a recurring space in my life. I turned to leave and thought I heard her whisper something into my ear. It sounded like, 'You will be my little goddess… my Bhairavi.'

My musical memories began before Dhondutai, with a woman called Sita-behn who came home to teach my mother light ragas and melodic bhajans when I was very young. I also remember a man coming over to teach my father how to play the tabla, before business worries took over and the rhythms of his life changed.

Both my parents belonged to business backgrounds. Sons were trained to take over the family business and daughters were groomed to find husbands. Girls were taught music or dance to enhance their marriage prospects. So, when Sita-behn, my mother's old music teacher, recommended a music school for me, I was promptly sent across.

I spent several tortured months at Sangeet Vidyalaya. It was located in the heart of Gamdevi, one of the oldest neighbourhoods in Bombay, occupied by old-timers who harbored a curious ambivalence—part disdain and part envy—towards people like me. For we were Bombay's brown sahibs, more comfortable watching a derivative Neil Simon than a masterpiece written in the local language. I went to an Anglican school, where we learned to speak the Queen's English and to speak broken Hindi with a self-conscious accent. Marathi was taught as a third language. We viewed it as a crude, amusing dialect that had to be learned so that you could communicate with the cleaning lady or cajole a local policeman into not giving you a fine.

The faculty of the music school in Gamdevi consisted of the Ranade sisters, an enterprising triumvirate who had spent several decades churning out batch after batch of uninspired singers. Each sat in a room that opened onto a balcony overlooking a noisy street. The first room was for the beginners, usually a cluster of giggling girls who were taught the basics of raga music from a set of textbooks (consisting of parts I, II and III). The second room was for those who managed to graduate from the first room. The third room, at the far end and one I rarely entered, was where the oldest Miss Ranade taught a select group of senior students.

On the first day, I sat in the first room, in a circle of girls, before one of the Ranade siblings and her creaking harmonium. She asked each of us to state our name and our favorite raga. Two of the girls had been named after ragas by their parents. The first, a dimpled thing in a floral cotton dress, coyly said in Marathi, 'My name is Bageshree and my favorite raga is Bageshree.' Every one laughed heartily and clapped. We then met Poorvi. Luckily her favorite raga was Malkaus. I had been growing increasingly nervous about my response and felt bits of breakfast flying about wildly in my stomach as we went through the circle and came closer to my turn. When all eyes rested on me expectantly, I forgot to mention my name and blurted out, 'Raga Yaman means Raga Bhairavi.'

I had meant to say, 'Raga Yaman and Raga Bhairavi,' but my eager attempt to speak Marathi translated into this indecipherable response, which set off a chorus of giggles. Even the teacher laughed.

Never before had I felt so conspicuously out of place; I was a foreigner in this traditional, Marathi-speaking music universe, and I was a mildly eccentric character in my pseudo English world, where young girls were more preoccupied with the length of their badminton skirts than with mystifying musical outposts tucked away in the city's dodgiest neighbourhoods.

I was mortified about going to the music class and regularly tried to come up with creative excuses for missing it. But stomach aches and homework didn't quite cut it with my mother. I succeeded once, when I managed to lock myself into the bathroom; by the time the locksmith was called to wrench open the door, class time was over. I hated my mother for pushing me into this embarrassing, depressing world. Besides the classes, I was routinely dragged to even more irksome music concerts, where I would usually fall asleep and wake up when the singer was rendering fast, arpeggiated passages which meant the end of the show was near.

Yet, like most reluctant students, I did manage to learn some music by default. At the Gamdevi music school, I got a basic introduction to the ragas. We were taught the grammar for each raga—how to go up the notes and then come down—followed by a simple, manicured composition. We learned one raga every two weeks and then rapidly moved on to the next. The curriculum was unabashedly devoid of nuance; the idea was to build a repertoire, which would culminate in an examination and a certificate. This was Indian Classical Music 101.

My mother slowly caught on that this was not the place for me. She wanted me to learn music from a teacher who would devote time to me exclusively, to teach me the fundamentals of voice culture, coax the notes out gradually, and instill depth in each utterance. Someone mentioned Dhondutai Kulkarni, who had recently moved to Bombay. Dhondutai belonged to the Jaipur Gharana, a spectacularly intellectual school of music, and was the only student of the legendary singer Kesarbai Kerkar.

My mother went to hear Dhondutai perform at the Bhulabhai Institute, an intimate concert hall tucked away on the first floor of a sea-facing building. Dhondutai started in a no-nonsense manner, right on time, with Lalita-Gauri, a compound raga that interweaves two ragas, Lalit and Gauri. Her music was highly complex. There was perfection, but as a critic had once noted 'not enough pain.' 'Sometimes, you don't listen to music for pleasure; you want to experience the pathos that stirs the soul.' Perhaps my mother liked the uncomplicated nature of Dhondutai's full-throated singing. She decided, into the second half of the concert, that she wanted her to be my music teacher.

In those days, there was a marvellous singer, Durgatai, whom my parents loved. But they felt that, while she may have been India's Maria Callas, Durgatai would not be the right teacher for their restless daughter. She was reputed to be somewhat inflammable. Legend had it that she had once flung a tabla at a student when he hit the wrong note for the third time in a row. She was a star performer, but a terrible mentor. Dhondutai, though not as famous, would be gentle and nurturing.

Our worlds were fated to collide. And so that is how I ended up, uncomfortable yet intrigued, sitting in my guru's modest home. What was to follow was a lifetime of learning—and not just of music.

Two

I went back to Kennedy Bridge the following week. In our first lesson, Dhondutai asked me to shut my eyes and listen to the singer's loyal accompanist, the tanpura. I was intrigued by the instrument, which looks like a sitar but plays just four notes over and over again. She ran her fingers over the strings and a hypnotic rhythmic drone started to fill the room. It created a constant murmur of serenity. Soon, all the ambient sounds—the whirring of the fan, the soft tick-tock of the table clock, the occasional shouts from children or vendors outside, Ayi's gentle snoring, the hissing of the pressure cooker from the kitchen—found their place against this background drone. From then on, the language we heard and spoke was that of music.

I started with the first note, sa. On that first day, to my dismay, Dhondutai made me sing only the base note—the tonal pillar of Indian music which remains unchanged, constant, reliable, and stoically oblivious to the whims and fancies of other notes. It is the foundation, the first and last note, the point at which the circle begins and ends. Within the boundaries of sa, one can play out all of life's dramas and moods. But every time one gets back to it, there is a sense of closure—like coming home after a long and exciting journey.

'Make the sound of your sa merge into the sa of the tanpura until both are one and you can't tell the difference,' said Dhondutai. 'Sa encompasses all the notes, just as pure white light contains all the colors of the rainbow.'

We finished our lesson in half an hour, a nod to my age and restless spirit. Dhondutai put the tanpura back in its resting place against the wall and shuffled into the kitchen. I followed her there, overwhelmed with curiosity. The kitchen was a dark space with a single, small window that looked out onto a courtyard in the center of the building. Dhondutai's entire culinary equipment fitted into a compact wooden cupboard in one corner. She pulled out a small, old-fashioned brass vessel and rinsed it.

A heavy-set woman, with a shocking white bob-cut and a dark face embedded with tributaries of suffering, emerged from the flat's other bedroom. It was the landlady, from whom my teacher had rented her room and the right to use the kitchen and bathroom. Dhondutai introduced me to Mausi, affectionately referring to me as 'her little student'. Mausi smiled and held her hand out to me limply and I shook it, both of us mildly uncomfortable with this western mode of greeting. I noticed her feathery moustache which she had trimmed unevenly, leaving behind bits of white stubble.

Dhondutai asked if I wanted tea, which I declined. As she started making it, she chattered on, and I stood next to her, leaning on the kitchen counter, listening.

'Making tea is a lesson in life,' she said. 'You think that you've made the tea just because you've put the kettle on the pot and dumped tea leaves into it. But take a deeper look at what's going on. Actually, someone has grown the tea leaves, someone else has pruned them, some poor fellow put them into packages. Someone has milked a cow and another has pressed sugar cane to give you sugar. And it is thanks to the fire that you can boil your water. So what you have done is a small speck in the scheme of tea-making. Never feel undue pride, for there is much more unseen energy contributing to your so-called achievement. What do you say, Mausi?'

'You are quite right, tai. It is all in God's hands,' said Mausi with a sigh, dabbing with the end of her sari the film of sweat misting her face from the steamy tea. Dhondutai laughed and poured the hot tea into two slightly chipped china cups and brought them into her room for her mother and herself. Ayi picked up the cup with a quivering hand, and spilled most of the tea on to the ground. She looked up at us like a sheepish child.

'Why can't you be a little more careful, Ayi?' scolded Dhondutai. 'How do you expect me to keep cleaning up after you? Here, give me that cup.' She shook her head and sighed. 'You didn't get burned did you?' Her voice softened and she went out to get a rag. Mausi walked in from the kitchen and gave Ayi a don't-worry smile. Ayi was looking at the floor. She slowly lay back on her bed and turned her face to the wall.

It was a touching scene. Three women in this tiny apartment, each with her own struggles and stories, supporting each other with empathy. One's face spoke of unhappiness, a husband who must have died in debt, leaving her a dark, peeling flat, half of which she had to rent out to keep from going hungry. The second had to cope with the shame of watching her body gradually detach itself from her mind.

The third was living with the pressure of knowing that she was born to deliver a creative gift to the world—and that her mission had not been accomplished. For, there were always medicines to buy and dinner to be made. Life was a constant struggle between mundane chores and her unworldly art.

I went back to the music room under Kennedy Bridge a couple of days later. I was disgruntled over missing out on my play time, but there was a part of me that was secretly curious to see Ayi and Mausi and the dollhouse again.

My next few lessons continued to revolve around the foundation note, sa. The repeated chanting of a single note, as if it were a mantra, is supposed to help the singer drown out all the distracting noises in her head. It centers the body, mind, and soul and brings them into equilibrium. It draws the breath into a steady rhythm. For this reason, we never made it to the six other notes or swaras. Instead of explaining all this to me, Dhondutai simply said that before going any further, I had to first please the spirit that resided in this swara.

Swara means note literally, but it holds a deeper significance than its western definition. It is not just a particular musical frequency that can be found by hitting the right key on a piano or plucking a string a particular way. It is not a mechanical pitch, but rather, an utterance that comes from deep within the human body.

The fundamental grammar of western and Indian music is built on the same seven notes—Indian music's sa, re, ga, ma, pa, dha and ni corroborate with the European heptatonic scale of do, re, mi, fa, so, la, ti—but as one begins to examine these notes and unravel the music they make, profound differences emerge between the two systems. These differences mirror the opposing thought processes that drive the west and the east.

The ancient western position on music was that it was

made up of patterns of sound with regular melodic intervals which reflect the simple ratios by which the world is organized and make sense to our organs of perception. Western theory is thus built around perceptible, rational ideas which the human mind can see, recognize, and find proof for.

Indian music is rooted in a fundamentally different assumption—that there is a continuous, unseen, and constantly changing reality which is the backdrop for all human action and perception. It is what shapes our karma or destiny, and helps explain why seemingly inexplicable things happen to us. The notes in Indian music are thus not categorical, separate, self-contained entities, but are connected through a subtle, elusive continuum of notes that can barely be identified by the human ear. They are, in the metaphysical sense, part of that reality which lies beyond perception. These in-between notes are called srutis, and they are the essence of Indian music.

In a very literal sense, these srutis are the half notes and quarter notes that fill the intervals between two notes. But that would be a grossly incomplete description. There is much more to the sruti, for it can entirely change the reality of the notes. For instance, how you reach a particular note is as important as the note itself. It may be arrived at from below, or above, after caressing that hidden note that hovers next to it, and it will evoke a completely different sensation than if the musician were to meet the note directly.

This explains why Indian music cannot be learned from textbooks. It has to be taught by a guru who can explain these nuances, coax the right note out of the student and help her achieve it. How would even the most articulate text manage to explain that you have to meet the swara gradually and lovingly and with a touch of foreplay?

The ancient scriptures were preserved in the oral tradition, where each phrase and utterance was memorized through a complex set of mnemonics and then recited with great emphasis on delivery, so that future generations got it just right. Yoga, also an ancient and secret discipline, was passed down from teacher to student, not through textbooks. The Indian classical musical tradition relies on a similar oral tradition where the teacher is a key player and often viewed with the same reverence with which one would treat a priest or a monk.

But there is only so much that can be taught. It is finally up to the student to understand the secrets of swara. The singer may have perfect pitch but may or may not get to the next level. It is only when the student gets a feel for the notes that her music will truly shine forth.

Singing has often been linked with divinity. According to Islamic mythology, Allah commanded his angels to make a clay statue of one of the saints, Hazrat Adam Alehos Salam. They did so, but when they tried to put the saint's soul in, it wouldn't stay—so, the merciful Allah asked them to sit inside the statue and sing. As soon as the singing began, the soul entered the statue, and the angels quickly locked it inside. This is why all humans, birds and beasts enjoy music—because they are made of the same clay.

Hindu musicians have their own interpretation of music's origins. They believe that the first element to emerge, long before life populated the universe, was the sound om, which embodies that universal spirit some call God. Perhaps this is why the sensation experienced, both for the artist and the connoisseur, when a musician enunciates the swara in its ultimate and precise form, is very similar to the feeling one has when one sits in a quiet temple, church, or mausoleum, and experiences that sudden epiphany.

Three

Most days, I hated the idea of going for my music lesson. After an exhausting day at school, I had to catch a bus to Kennedy Bridge with my old Nepalese ayah Bhakti Maya in tow—when I could be relaxing at a girlfriend's house or playing kitchen-kitchen in the garden; this involved crushing leaves and stones into little imaginary dishes, and serving them to the obliging building watchman. It was not just the boredom of repeating the same note for an hour, but also the terror I secretly faced each time I navigated the area around my teacher's home.

The bus dropped us off on the bridge. We then went down a flight of eroded stairs to get to the road on which Dhondutai lived. Bombay's stairways hang like a kind of nowhere territory between two definitive spaces such as roads or platforms, and they have become havens for the marginalized: beggars pick their favorite set of stairs and settle down there for years, drug addicts hide their needles in crevices on the landings, and the sloping underside sometimes doubles as a roof for a homeless family. The stairs of Kennedy Bridge harboured not just the usual flotsam, but also a couple of creepy pimps who hovered around smoking cigarettes, trying to catch an early customer. One pock-faced man in particular was usually around when I got there, and felt compelled to throw a lurid remark at me when I walked by.

'Come with me, sweetie?' he would sneer, without fail. Once, he had brushed against my eleven-year-old breasts and left me nauseous with fear and shame. But my near-blind ayah, Bhakti, doddering behind me, scarcely caught on to what was going on, for a blob of tobacco hidden deep inside her cheek had long deadened her senses to life's unpleasant realities. I ran down the stairs at full speed, without looking behind, and stopped only when I had entered Dhondutai's building. A few minutes later, Bhakti Maya came up to me, panting, and reprimanded me for running off like that. She was allowed to do that. Bhakti Maya had come to work with my family as part of my mother's dowry and stayed on until she died, twenty-five years later.

Once I entered Dhondutai's home, I felt I was in a cocoon of comfort—and I know Bhakti sensed it too.

I had now started having lessons on Saturday mornings as well. The first morning I got there, I was surprised at how the neighbourhood changed its mood from that of the evening. The road was much quieter and the pimps probably asleep. I arrived while Dhondutai was still in the middle of her morning prayers.

Her room smelt ambrosial, like a temple at dawn. Dhondutai sat in front of the altar, freshly bathed, in a baby pink sari. She motioned for me to sit next to her while she continued muttering her mantras in a sing-song drone. She was rubbing a stick of sandalwood against a round tablet in a circular motion, periodically sprinkling water on it, so that the stick disintegrated into a paste. Every few minutes she swept up the paste with her index finger and put it into a miniature silver plate.

I was more mesmerized by the elaborate ritual than I would have been sitting in front of a real, made-in-Switzerland dollhouse. Dhondutai picked up the silver gods and placed them in a large bowl. They were then doused with water. She lifted each god, rubbed it with a towel, and placed it back in the altar where it sparkled softly. It was time now for the fragrant sandalwood. With her middle finger, she dabbed a tiny blob of the creamy ochre paste on to each of the figurines. She did the same thing with the red kumkum and yellow turmeric powder. She then unraveled a large green leaf which had been folded like a wrapper and tied with a string. Inside, lay a bunch of flowers and petals. She picked them up, one at a time, and placed the fresh purple, pink and crimson offerings before each of the statues. The ornamentation was complete. The figures looked resplendent.

I had seen my grandmother praying and performing her version of the same ritual. But never before had I seen such tenderness. To Dhondutai, these were not lifeless idols or distant celestial beings, but little people, who needed to be bathed, dressed, loved and remembered just as one would a child or an old parent. These were her daily companions.

It was now time to chant the prayers out loud, the final commemoration. Dhondutai poured oil into a little silver lamp which was waiting patiently with its wick erect. She lit the lamp, and rotated it in front of the altar while reciting her prayers. Half an hour later, we were done. As she got up slowly from the prayer mat, wincing at the pain in her leg, she said, 'Faith is everything you know… If you have faith, nothing can touch you.'

She continued softly, 'You are lucky because you get to sing in front of all the gods and they love music. You will always be blessed. That is what has protected me all these years.' She told me about Haridas Swami, a saint-singer, a story she would repeat to me many times over the years because it touched on the difference between music and great music.

Mia Tansen was a singer from the sixteenth century. He was called the father of Hindustani classical music, and a number of ragas have been named after him. No one could match his style or his repertoire. When the emperor Akbar heard his music, he instantly inducted him into his royal court, and Tansen was named one of the nine gems of the empire.

One day, as they were strolling through the palace rose gardens, discussing music, Akbar said to him, 'Tansen, you sing so magnificently. Who taught you this music? Your teacher must be even better than you. Who is he? Why haven't we heard him yet?'

Tansen smiled and said, 'Come I will show you. But be prepared for a long journey.'

Akbar ordered his men to bring his disguise. Every so often, the emperor would wear the clothes of a common man and wander into his kingdom to get a feel for what was going on. Today, he dressed like a wood-cutter. The two of them got on their horses and rode out towards the edge of the city. There, they left their horses at a resthouse, and began to walk into a dense forest. It was several hours before they came to a clearing next to a brook. Akbar suggested that they sit down and rest. They lay down by the water, and allowed themselves to be enveloped by the sounds of nature. The emperor drifted off into a sweet slumber.

He woke up dreamily to the sound of singing such as he'd never heard before. The notes of Raga Malkauns filled the air and seemed to be in perfect harmony with the sound of the water, the rustle of the leaves and the cry of the cuckoo. Akbar lay in wonder for a few minutes and murmured, 'Subhanallah! This is a dialogue with the divine.'

He then jumped up and started walking towards the music. He saw Tansen standing, as if in a trance, next to a great banyan tree. The singer beckoned the king to follow him. The notes came closer and closer, as they walked towards the singing. Then, just when the last note fell gently, they saw a hut. A man was sitting in the porch, his eyes shut. He wore a simple muslin dhoti, nothing else. He looked towards the duo and said, 'Welcome, Akbar.'

'How did you know it was me?' replied the king.

The man, Haridas Swami merely smiled and invited them inside.

On their way back, they were silent most of the way. Then, Akbar asked Tansen, 'If he can sing like that, why can't you?'

Tansen said, 'That's simple, dear king. I sing for you. He sings for God.'

'So, you see,' said Dhondutai, as she started tuning the tanpura, carefully twisting the knobs at the end of the stem. 'Once you forget yourself and the world around you, once you dismiss all the rewards and recognition you could be getting for your art, and sing only as a form of meditation, your music will break free. You also begin to know things that other people don't know. Truths reveal themselves to you. That is how Haridas Swami could see through Akbar's disguise right away. It comes from living in solitude and meditating only on music. I have experienced it too.'

I looked at her quizzically, but my eyes had already wandered to the little bowl of prasada that lay in front of the altar. Every day, the bowl contained some new treat— shevi, brown threads of caramelized bliss, kheer, or halwa. Today was carrot halwa with a sprinkling of crushed almonds.

'Tomorrow is Janmashtami, the birthday of Krishna. Come, let's take a short break from practicing sa and I will teach you a song about Krishna and Radha playing holi. The colored powder they fling at each other is a metaphor for love… not physical love, you know. This is the universal love that you will slowly grow to understand.'

I realized many years later that Dhondutai lived in a parallel universe somewhat removed from the one we traversed, where everything translated into a musical metaphor. If it was Krishna's birthday, we would learn a song praising him. When the monsoons came around, it was time to sing Raga Megh or Malhar, which herald the rain. If there was a wedding in the family, we would learn the heroic Raga Shahana and a composition which described the bride and groom in their finery. There was this wonderful synchronicity of thought, action and sound, where the most mundane ritual was translated into a musical idiom. She hummed while she cooked, in slow cadences. She taught me how even the vegetable-seller, who went from building to building and let out a sing-song wail announcing her arrival, had perfect pitch.

At the time, though, my thoughts were more imme-diate. I had already run into the kitchen to return with three saucers for the halwa that lay glistening before the altar. Mausi came in from the other room to sample the offering and Bhakti was invited to partake of it as well. Prasada is God's food, it does not recognize class. I handed Ayi a plate and we both sat and devoured the sweet orange flakes that floated in ghee like a spray of fresh marigolds on the Ganges.

Four

It was when I had belted out sa a couple of hundred times, and squirmed and squinted the same number of times along the way, that we moved on to the other notes—not the entire seven, but a specific combination of five notes which is the melodic framework for Raga Bhoop.

'I know you are getting bored. I'm going to teach you Bhoop which you will find quite enjoyable,' Dhondutai told me one evening. The raga would become my soulmate for the next two years.

Bhoop is one of the most popular ragas in the musical treasury. The reason Dhondutai selected this raga to initiate me was because it is simple in structure and form. The beauty of Bhoop lies in being able to create numerous permutations and combinations with just five notes. The absent notes are as important as the notes which are being sung.

Dhondutai ignored the fact that I had learned seven or eight ragas from the beleaguered Miss Ranade in the Gamdevi school, because knowing the scale of a raga did not mean knowing how to sing it. Besides, according to her, very few others were qualified to sing, let alone teach. We started from scratch and I was thus initiated into that wonderful, ancient system called the guru-shishya parampara.

The way Miss Ranade, with her little textbooks, had taught us was certainly one way of looking at ragas—hers was not an incorrect approach, merely incomplete. It allowed one to take a dip in the ocean and experience its buoyancy, but scarcely imagine its depth.

There are several hundred known ragas, and many more that have fallen out of public consciousness over the years.

A raga is a melodic framework or a defined set of notes—there have to be at least five—taken from the seven-note scale. It has a specific ascending and descending scale. There can be one or two dominant notes, to which the melody keeps returning. They are like the raga's spokespersons. There may also be a specific phrase, a defining motif, which instantly evokes that particular raga. Another characteristic is that it is sung in a particular octave area. Some ragas concentrate on the lower end, others on the higher register. So, two ragas could have the same set of notes, but the manner in which they are rendered, could make them sound completely different.

This framework of notes and scales are the raga's broad parameters. The charm lies in finding freedom within the discipline. However, you must not trespass beyond the boundaries of the raga, or you will risk a hiss of disapproval from the discerning listener. For instance, in raga Mian-ki-Todi, you can only get to pa after touching the note above, dha, and you must comply with that idiom every time pa figures in the composition.

That is the literal definition of a raga. It will get you past the university music exam and even perhaps secure you a radio audition. The national broadcasting networks require that you know fifteen or twenty ragas and be able to sing neat compositions in each of them reasonably well. Thousands of musicians have been able to get by with that.

But there is an entirely different aspect to a raga, just as a poem is much more than a collection of words. Raga's etymological roots are found in the word ranga, which means color. A raga must evoke a color, an emotional reaction.

There is a deep link between a raga and human emotion which has been documented in the *Natyashastra*, one of the earliest texts on the performing arts. This ancient document describes the eight moods to which all performance is linked. They are: erotic, compassionate, comic, angry, heroic, terrible, odious and wondrous. Specific combinations and patterns of notes supposedly evoke one or other of these emotional fields. The most popular ragas are those that conjure up the erotic or the compassionate states—like Raga Bhairavi, which has hosted numerous compositions on love and longing.

While these links are not to be taken too literally, the idea is that ragas are not merely abstract aesthetic constructs, but are connected to emotions, events, even seasons. They are linked to man's wider social and cultural universe.

'To understand and perform the raga in its true sense requires life-long meditation on the notes—and on yourself,' Dhondutai told me. 'Merely mastering the notes is not enough. You have to reflect on the human condition, on life itself. Every time I sing a raga, it unfolds and expands, revealing new insights and pathways. That is why they say that a musician really becomes a musician at the end of his life. It is only once you can use the notes to tell a greater story that you are floating in that bottomless ocean.'

Many years later, when I was able to grasp the nuances of swara and raga, I started to understand what Dhondutai meant when she said, 'Every swara has several srutis, which are the subtle shades within the note. For example, the note ma in Raga Yaman lies in the uppermost sruti, the one closest to pa. It is only when you start hitting the precise sruti of the raga that the raga will open up to you and say, "Aah! Now you may enter me… "'

Five

'Sing each note as long as you can hold it. Then build it up to two notes at a time, then three, four... now all five. Slightly faster, this time. Go all the way up and down in one breath. This time, up and down six times without stopping for breath. Excellent! Try fitting in one more cycle. If you start each round with a slight jerk, you will get momentum and more control over your breath... That's right... Shaabaash beta, good job!'

At the time, I could scarcely understand the complexity of what I was learning. Dhondutai made me blindly master the grammar of this music through little techniques and stories to keep my interest going. She created fun competitions to get me to stretch my limits. For instance, each time I sang a note, I would take a deep breath and begin, and she would start counting the seconds that I could hold it, urging me to extend it just a little longer. If I faltered in between and went slightly off-key, she would stop me and ask me to start again. When it came to the faster cycles, I would make little bets with myself. If I could fit in one more round without taking a breath, then it meant that the new boy in class liked me!

Besides establishing the integrity of the notes in the raga, Dhondutai was initiating me into the secrets of voice culture that she had learned from her teachers. I was learning how to throw my voice and exercise breath control—two integral and distinguishing characteristics of the Jaipur school of music. It amused me that she revealed these basics about voice culture to me as if they were state secrets, not to be disclosed to any random person.

'Most singers sing from up here,' Dhondutai said, pointing to her throat. 'But the secret of our singing is that you must sing from your navel. Throw your voice such that you should never need a microphone. The person sitting in the last row of the hall should be able to distinguish every single note in your taan.'

For this reason, the singer's posture matters. I was told that I must sit cross-legged with my back straight so that the notes would be aligned with the body's chakras, and could come through without faltering. In fact, she made sure that our lessons took place in front of a mirror so that I could correct myself every time I slouched.

Who would imagine that such a simple exercise—establishing my posture—would take so much out of my unsuspecting music teacher. This was one of the first instances when our two worlds did not meet. For Dhondutai, sitting cross-legged on the floor was easy. It was how traditional Indians ate their meals, read, or relaxed. I, on the other hand, had eaten my meals at a dining table. The idea of sitting cross-legged was charming, but not easily achieved given the pins and needles that would set in at the soles of my feet within five minutes.

Thus, many of our initial lessons revolved around her scolding me for fidgeting and shifting, while I moved from the cross-legged position to a side-kneel, and once even to stretch my legs in front of me and do a quick, impudent toe-curl. This was one of the rare occasions when she reprimanded me. 'You can't do that. Never point your feet towards your guru and, more importantly, never in front of the tanpura. It is the worst insult to the goddess of music.'

In those moments, Ayi, sitting silently in the corner of the room, watching the proceedings, would jump to my rescue and say, 'Why are you bothering the poor girl so much? She's still young. Let her be.'

'Don't interfere. Are you teaching her or am I?' Dhondutai would retort.

Ayi would then mumble something back and Dhondutai would scold her but it was always a feeble admonishment. The old woman and I would exchange sly glances and I knew I had won.

Ayi and I shared that unique bond which can only exist between a child and an old person, for both prefer to live life in a two-dimensional cartoon strip which has no tolerance for the practical world. She only spoke Marathi, and I was most comfortable in English, but we shared little secrets. We had something else in common. We were both slightly afraid of Dhondutai's disciplinarian ways.

'Ayi look what I got you,' I whispered to her one evening, when Dhondutai was out of sight in the kitchen. The old lady's face showed a flicker of interest, as I came up to her and opened a little box of marzipan sweets under her nose. Ayi chuckled and picked up a sugary pink rose. She nibbled at its edges, then popped the whole thing in her mouth. I chose the green tulip and licked its petals, watching her with delight.

'I picked these up on the way back from school at the Parsi Dairy. We were so-oo bored in school today. They cancelled our PE class, so we had to sit and do more maths...' I chattered on and Ayi nodded back. After a while, too tired to sit up, she lay down and fell asleep like an infant. I looked at her and wondered what old people dreamt about.

Most of the time, Ayi was either sitting on her bed, vaguely watching what was going on in the room, or lying on her side, staring at the wall with one hand folded under her head. She would spend long hours on her side, facing the pale green blankness. Sometimes, her finger traced a pattern on the wall and then fell gently to her side as she fell asleep. She rarely went out of the house because there was really nowhere to go. After a while, it became difficult for her to walk even to the bathroom, and definitely impossible for her to sit on her haunches. So, Dhondutai bought a wooden chair with a removable tinny toilet pan. This lay shamefacedly in a corner of the room, and Ayi was forced to swallow her pride and watch helplessly as her daughter cleaned up after her.

Dhondutai was out vegetable shopping one evening, when I arrived for my lesson. Ayi beckoned to me to come and sit down and Mausi came in from the kitchen to keep me company as well, dabbing her brow with the end of her sari. There was always a film of sweat on her face.

They chatted with each other in Marathi, while Bhakti Maya, who was just about entering her tobacco-induced stupor, sat at her usual place by the doorway, and added her own sympathetic hisses and grunts to the conversation. I sat swinging my legs on the sofa-bed, not particularly unhappy over the fact that I was missing a lesson.

'Did you know how Dhondutai got her unusual name?' Mausi suddenly asked me, in Hindi.

'No.' My interest was stirred. I had been desperate to find out why my teacher had a name that was more suited for a pet puppy. Dhondu! I looked at Ayi and thought I saw her eyes cloud over with nostalgia.

'Ayi has been through so much, you cannot even imagine it,' said Mausi, shaking her head.

It was the early 1920s in a small town called Kolhapur, a few hundred miles south and inland from Bombay. A pretty young woman, barely eighteen, who was called Sonatai long before she became Ayi, had just given birth to a baby girl. The family was overjoyed and celebrated by hosting a feast for the Brahmins in the vicinity.

In those days, Ayi's younger brother, a boy of ten, lived with them. He always wanted to pick up the baby and play with her, but was not allowed to do so. One evening, the baby was fast asleep in her cot, and Ayi decided to nip out and visit the temple. She told her brother to keep an eye on the baby and not to disturb her. The boy happily agreed. A few minutes after his sister left, he picked up the gas lantern and tiptoed into the room where his niece was sleeping. As he leaned over the cot and watched the tiny creature with fascination, the lantern slipped and a piece of bedding caught fire. Within seconds, the crib was in flames. The boy was so mortified that he stood there, paralyzed as he watched the flames slowly envelope the bed. It was only when the neighbours saw black smoke billowing out of the window that they came running in. By then it was too late.

Ayi's second child, a boy, died almost immediately after birth, of pneumonia. When she had her third baby, a girl, the family decided that they would do whatever they could to protect her. Her grandmother insisted that they name her Dhondu. It means stone.

In those days, parents would have their little boys' ears pierced to disguise them so that the devil would not carry them away, for the devil didn't care for girls. Since this was a girl, the only thing they could think of was to give her a strange, almost repulsive name which would put the evil spirits off. This was how Dhondutai arrived into this world, wailing in perfect pitch, carrying with her a promise of something unusual and special.

Six

One of Dhondutai's favorite stories about tutelage was about the founder of the Jaipur school of music, Alladiya Khan, who was born in the late nineteenth century.

'The Khansahib was a young man, still under training with his uncle Jahangir Khan,' said Dhondutai. 'You haven't heard of Jahangir Khan? When he sang, it was as if monumental columns of notes stood before the listener,' she continued, standing in front of the mirror and squinting, as she painted a perfectly round bindi on her forehead.

She continued the story, putting her little cosmetic stick back in its allocated corner in the cupboard. The young Alladiya had given one of his first performances and surprised everyone with his talent. He, his teacher, and some other musicians were walking back after the concert, late at night. Alladiya was high from his heady performance, the others from guzzling down the music along with a few goblets of wine. They kept praising him and calling him 'the new khansahib'. Jahangir Khan listened to the banter for a while, then turned to his nephew, slapped him across his face, and said, 'You could have sung better.'

'It wasn't that he was unhappy with Alladiya's performance,' said Dhondutai. 'But in those days, elders believed that too much praise at an early an age could ruin you. Times have really changed,' she added, with a sigh. 'You people have it too good. There is no discipline, too much freedom. When I was young…'

This was her regular mantra. I usually responded by looking bored and humming to myself, or by smiling cheekily and rolling my eyes, or by staring at the patterns on the carpet and pretending not to listen…

'… And these Parsis. Whatever you say, they are different from us.'

I looked up, surprised. Dhondutai's diatribe was not directed at me this time, but at another student, a recent addition to her music school. I sat up and became more attentive while my teacher berated the new victim. Her name was Delna, and she was a pale Parsi girl with a sprinkling of pink acne, who smelt faintly of fish and talcum powder. Her father, Dr Rustom Doctor, was a loyal devotee of music.

Parsi homes generally feature grandfather clocks, grand pianos and, almost always, a wedding portrait of the queen of England. But, unlike most Parsis, whose loyalties lay with Bach and Zubin Mehta, Dr Rustom worshipped Firoz Dastur, who happened to be Parsi, but had transgressed and become a Hindustani classical singer.

Dr Rustom was a dentist and had been saving up for many years so that his daughter could learn Indian classical music. To be able to afford this indulgence, he had set up a special pediatric clinic on weekends and started visiting local schools, giving lectures on oral hygiene so that he could impress parents and get them to send their children to him. I was one of his patients. When he found out that I was learning music, he immediately asked me how he could get in touch with my teacher. After extracting a promise that he would never bother me about my cavities, I gave him Dhondutai's whereabouts.

Dr Rustom took Delna to Dhondutai. She was a diligent student, but never made it beyond the rudiments of Raga Bhoop. Dr Rustom's heartfelt enthusiasm touched Dhondutai and she didn't have the heart to tell him that his daughter profoundly lacked a sense of pitch.

'This has been my dream,' he revealed to her in his staccato, Parsi-accented Hindi.

'She is very attentive, but doctor...'

'Some day, when I am old and retired, I would like to shut my eyes and just listen to my daughter sing to me.'

'Of course, of course, but...' and then she stopped, unable to break his heart.

He would reminisce about the days when his father took him to Firoz Dastur's Grant Road home. Grant Road, which has since decayed like a neglected tooth, was then a vibrant neighbourhood in which a number of old Parsi families lived. As a young boy, the doctor had spent many Sunday afternoons walking up the rickety stairs to Firoz Dastur's flat, where he listened to the old masters on a cranky gramophone beneath a portrait of the great singer Abdul Karim Khan.

The doctor was a very kind man and insisted on taking Ayi to his clinic to fix her a set of customized dentures. But after a heart-wrenching year of getting his darling Delna to hit re without infringing on ga, Dhondutai could take it no more.

'It pierces every bone in my body when she kills the note,' Dhondutai said to me that morning, shuddering and holding a hand to her ear. 'The doctor told me he would pay me double, or do whatever he could to keep her on, but

I am not interested. Why should I waste my time, and hers, if she is never going to be able to sing?'

I nodded with exaggerated sympathy, secretly delighted to participate in the demolition of a fellow student.

The five hundred extra rupees that came to her every month from cavity money meant nothing to Dhondutai. What was she going to buy? New furniture? She would have to pile it on top of the old. Saris, which would only crowd the solitary cupboard in the room? Gold jewellery for the children she had never had? It was useless. You could not bribe Dhondutai with anything other than a promise to sing well. So, she discontinued Delna and sent her back to her violin lessons with Miss Shirley Cowasji in Grant Road.

I met Delna a couple of months later when I went back to the dentist's clinic to get a cavity filled. She complained sadly about how Miss Shirley would pinch her because she didn't get the notes right. She missed Dhondutai.

But Dhondutai was adamant. She could not bear these lessons of mutual drudgery. She did not want any more incompetent students disrupting her peace of mind, and happily retreated to her solitary existence, with her old students—me, a pretty young girl called Rani, and one other much older woman, Manjutai.

It had rained incessantly for two days. But my music lesson was never cancelled. Dhondutai had stoic views on such things, and so did my mother. I felt like a helpless butterfly, crushed between these two strong women, as I ran through the brown, phlegmy puddles into Congress House. I trudged up the stairs, slightly wet despite dashing from the car. Dhondutai pulled out a thin, checkered towel hanging from a hook behind the door, and gave it to me. 'Here, wipe yourself before you catch a cold and pass it on to me,' she said with a laugh. Ayi smiled at the joke.

The towel smelled of her eucalyptus oil, and I cringed inwardly as I gave myself a quick wipe-down. Dhondutai handed me a type-written letter. 'Read what it says. You know my English isn't very good.'

It was an invitation requesting her to sing at a small auditorium in Matunga.

'Next month,' she declared, taking the letter back and putting it on the little blue table in the center of the room. 'And I want you to play the tanpura and accompany me on stage this time. You are ready for your public debut. Let them see my little Kesarbai.' She laughed and turned to her mother. 'Now let's see what those music critics say. They will be shocked when they hear this one. All she has to do is sing two or three taans and she will leave them gasping.'

A pang of nervousness slid through me so fast that I barely sensed it. I had just turned thirteen and had been learning Raga Bhoop for just over two years. My teacher was using me, her little prodigy, to settle old scores with the people who had dared to dismiss her talent in the cultural columns of the newspapers.

We started learning the new raga that she would be singing—Tilak Kamod, a lilting, almost playful raga. I remembered it from Miss Ranade's school and the notes resonated with me. She was careful to teach me the basic scale and then the two-three taans that were crafted to elicit reactions from the crowd. She would also sing Bhoop that day, just so that I could sing along with her. My lessons went well and Dhondutai's excitement grew with each passing day. My mother got me a new salwar-kameez especially for the show. It was a self-embossed canary yellow outfit with a contrasting black dupatta.

This may have triggered the disaster.

As soon as Dhondutai saw me enter the green room on the evening of the concert, she said, 'What is wrong with you? You are wearing black?'

I stared at her in fright and dismay, and suppressed the other big source of anxiety that was churning inside me. That morning, I had woken up to an ugly patch of wetness, my first period. She must have seen the fright on my face, for her tone suddenly became kinder and she told me to sit, while she continued to do her warm-up scales. How could I have realized then, that she too may have been nervous, and who else could she take it out on?

'Don't worry,' whispered Manjutai reassuringly. Although she was her student, Manjutai was much older than Dhondutai, and she looked upon her teacher's eccentricities with a mature detachment.

An hour later, as I sat behind my teacher on stage, strumming the tanpura, the combination of my inappropriate colors, my recent pubescence, and a hideous stiffness that had begun to creep up my foot, all conspired to make me intensely uncomfortable. When Dhondutai turned to me and gave me the signal to sing, I sang one of the taans I had practiced for the last three weeks. It came out pat. She nodded encouragingly and exclaimed to a man sitting in the front row, 'See?'

But the next time she turned to me, my foot was buzzing with pain, and the minute I opened my mouth, I knew I was off-key. I struggled through the half-notes, hearing myself deteriorate with each second. Before I had finished the piece, Dhondutai cut me off. She didn't allow me to sing again, and periodically looked to her other accompanist, Manjutai, for support, when she needed to take a breather or a sip of hot tea. I spent the rest of the evening in a cloud of pain and misery, desperate for the concert to end.

Two days later, when Dhondutai dissected the Matunga concert for her little audience at home—Mausi and Ayi—I was quite surprised at her selective memory. She seemed to have forgotten her anger and disappointment over my disastrous debut. Luckily for me, one music critic had come up to her and told her that he was very impressed with her singing. He had also said a few kind words about my voice. No matter how aloof she was from the world, such things did matter.

'Little Namita didn't sing her best, but after all this was her first time,' said Dhondutai, bringing in two cups of tea from the kitchen. 'She will learn from this and the next time, she will be better,' she added, smiling at me. 'I also remember when I used to get my monthly. I would sing a note on high, and it would come gushing down below.' Dhondutai chuckled, as she slurped tea from the saucer.

Mausi put her cup and saucer down. She looked at me and shook her head with a smile. 'Where will you find a teacher like this, my girl? She loves you more than a grandmother would. You are her lucky star.'

'But next time, please ask me what color to wear to a concert,' interjected Dhondutai, in a mock-stern voice. 'It is very important. We can do without the bad spirits. They are enough bad human beings floating around.'

She came and gave me a little hug and I felt like melting with embarassment.

47

I had begun to adore my teacher, though I disguised my feelings behind a mask of bemusement or nonchalance. I still refused to touch her feet, like most others did, because I found it awkward and beneath me to do so. For some reason, she didn't expect it from me.

But she knew I cared. Every so often, I brought her something which showed her how I really felt—like the little terracotta Ganesha statue that I had made in my pottery class for her and a painting of me playing the tanpura in the music room. If my mother was giving her a sari or a set of cushions on her birthday, I decorated the gift wrapping with flowers I had pressed. She would laugh with great amusement when she unraveled these little packages. The contents would find pride of place in her room. And I reveled in her happiness.

Ayi had been growing weaker and weaker and now barely got out of bed. She often did not have the energy to sit up and use the toilet chair next to her. Dhondutai and I would watch with dismay as a wet patch spread silently on the bed. I often helped her change the sheets.

One morning, Dhondutai came out of her bath to find her mother slumped on the arm of the toilet chair, breathing heavily, her eyes closed. She panicked. Mausi was out, visiting her daughter in her village. She ran to the neighbours to use their phone. She realized that even her little gods might not be able to help her this time. She had to call a doctor.

When I got there that afternoon, I knew something was amiss. She was praying loudly in front of the altar and the faux lamp seemed to be flickering with more vigour than usual. She beckoned to me to sit while she finished murmuring her prayers, then slowly got up and sat down next to Ayi and began pressing her head gently.

The medicines the doctor had recommended were expensive. Dhondutai had checked her bank passbook half-heartedly, but knew quite well that she would not have more than a few thousand rupees in savings. A concert had not come her way in many months and who knew when she would be invited next. Her fate lay in the hands of the music festival organizers and she was convinced they all conspired to keep her out of the limelight. There was only one way out. She turned to me.

'Beta, if you know of anyone who would like to take lessons from me, please call them.'

'Baiji, you can always sell your tanpuras if you need the money,' I replied, without thinking. My teacher's face grew white.

'Don't ever, ever utter such words again,' she said quietly. 'Do you realize this is my everything? This is all the wealth I have in the world? Do you have any idea?'

It was the first time I had seen my teacher break down. At that moment, I decided I would do whatever I could to help. 'I will definitely ask around. Baiji, don't worry. Everything will be fine.'

Dhondutai nodded silently, dabbing her eyes with her sari. She continued to sit next to her mother, and lifted her hand to signal the start of the lesson. 'Sa. Come now, sit up straight.'

It was the illness that initially brought Mandakini and Jane and Kuntatai into her life. For the first time ever, Dhondutai compromised, tucking away her ideals about the perfect student and the purity of teaching somewhere deep inside her. She became a teacher driven by the simple neccessity that inspired many of her contemporaries—money.

Mandakini was the boisterous and buxom daughter of an industrialist who made polyester garments. They were distantly related to my family. At sweet sixteen, Mandakini, or Mandy as she was called, was being primed to become the perfect wife. This meant dance class, baking class and bonsai. When I met Mandy's mother, at a wedding a few weeks later, I convinced her, over bowls of rich cashew ice cream, that if she added singing to her daughter's list of talents, she would be able to ensnare a groom even more eligible than the handsome young man getting married under the banana leaf in front of us. Promptly, Mandy was sent to learn music from Dhondutai.

'Not a bad voice,' exclaimed Dhondutai, hopefully, during the first lesson. Encouraged, the young girl didn't stop, revealing not only the quality of her voice, but also terrific stamina, nurtured on a diet of purified butter.

'Baiji, I would really love to learn songs about love,' said Mandy earnestly. For her, music was learned so as to oblige the indulgent aunt who would ask for a little drawing room performance after a dinner party.

Dhondutai frowned at her new student's forward request. She had barely begun and the notes had scarcely settled into her vocal chords. But she compromised, and said she would teach her a love song—though not quite what Mandy had in mind. It was set in Raga Yaman, another beginner's raga like Bhoop, and the composition dwelt on unrequited love.

'Pour more passion and sweet sorrow into the words,' cajoled Dhondutai. The girl had no idea what she was talking about.

But Mandakini was gifted with a rich and textured voice and was determined to learn music. Dhondutai even started harbouring dreams of turning her into a great singer, dreams which would be summarily crushed every time Mandy's mother came across to check on her daughter's progress, and Dhondutai was reminded that her student was only being prepared for the slaughterhouse. Meanwhile, I continued to be my teacher's agent and solicited anyone who had the remotest interest in what I began describing as a dying art form. I pulled in a curious menagerie of students that shook up Dhondutai's placid world. While her music school swelled in size, Ayi slowly recovered.

The most unlikely candidate was Jane, a classical violinist from England whose search for spiritual bliss had taken her into the cannabis-covered hills of Kulu-Manali and down the streets of Varanasi, and finally found an unexpected ending in this grimy heart of Bombay.

She was introduced to Dhondutai by my mother, who had met her through common friends in London. Jane's husband was a well-known painter who had just acquired a red haired mistress.

She arrived early one morning, causing a stir on the street, which was still rheumy-eyed from its late night escapades. Little boys stopped their game of marbles to stare at the six foot-tall white woman wearing an oversized, handspun kurta and a serene smile they couldn't quite place. Jane climbed the stairs, oblivious to the leprous walls and rotting garbage cans that lined her path. Dhondutai ushered her in, shooing away the train of children that had followed her upstairs, dancing and mimicking her walk. They greeted each other, hands folded.

'Nummer-stay,' ventured Jane, enunciating each syllable carefully.

'Please… do come in,' faltered Dhondutai, speaking in English.

Jane spoke no Hindi or Marathi, Dhondutai barely understood English, but over the next couple of months, they developed a unique language that was built around musical notes and phrases. Sa—base note, re—tension, a little pain, ga—back to equilibrium. 'Is this life itself?' Jane asked, taking a deep breath and rolling her eyes upwards, in an inspired moment.

Dhondutai admired Jane's tenacious desire to learn despite the cultural handicaps. Praising her, she later said to me, 'This is what we should take from the west—their work ethic and desire to succeed against all odds. Instead, we take the worst things from them, like their dress habits, their bad music.' I squirmed and giggled. I happened to be wearing my favorite stone-washed denim shorts that day and was listening to an Abba tape on my walkman.

A couple of bored housewives also showed up at her flat to learn music, but it was clear they harboured no pretensions of trying to become professional singers. A few hours of music was their only escape from bitter, balding husbands and dreary lives. They started and finished their music lesson in the same spot, week after week, without really getting anywhere. This was their therapy.

Dhondutai knew that these were hopeless cases with no musical future. But she also recognized the healing power of music and was willing to use it occasionally on someone who needed it. 'Music does something, not just our music but any kind of vocalization,' she explained to me once. 'The secret is that because it requires a fuller, free, and rhythmic breathing, it brings about a natural high. It is like meditation,' she said.

Without even knowing it, she was articulating the premise behind the new science of psycho-acoustics, which uses music to soothe nerves, even cure certain diseases. In the old days, physicians used to prescribe listening to ragas to cure diseases. Notes corresponded to different parts of the body. If someone had a problem with his liver, he was told to listen to Raga Shri because its dominant note, re, supposedly soothed the liver. According to legend, Orpheus, the Greek god of music, was able to calm wild beasts, make trees dance, and still rivers with sound. Dhondutai knew she had the power to change people's lives.

Dhondutai had begun to enjoy these interactions outside her otherwise solitary existence, and her new students had their uses. One of the women, Kuntatai, was so unhappy with her insurance salesman husband, demonic mother-in-law and wastrel son—all of whom lived together in a matchbox apartment in Mira Road, a miserable suburb on the outskirts of Bombay—that she had resorted to conjuring up her own parallel private world; she become a self-professed clairvoyant. Once, when Mausi lost a gold chain which she had carefully stashed away in the folds of a petticoat deep inside her cupboard, Dhondutai advised her to run to the neighbour's house and call Kuntatai.

'Hello, hello, is that Kuntatai?' Mausi clutched the phone receiver with both hands desperately.

'You have lost something…' the voice reproached on the other end. Kuntatai was speaking in a monotonous drone, as if in a trance. 'It is down… look down.' The phone went dead. Mausi stared at the handset. Then, she put it down, feeling confused. She later found the gold chain curled up in a dust ball under the cupboard.

One of the few times all the students came together was on Guru Purnima, the day after a full moon in July when students around the country formally acknowledge their teachers with flowers and gifts. That year, Dhondutai's newfound group flocked into the little flat in the morning, carrying gifts and sweets and hoping to get a blessing in return. Jane brought a perfume and a box of diabetic chocolates picked up on a recent trip home. Mandy presented her with a startlingly fuschia silk sari. Kuntatai brought a silver lamp for the altar. Others came with a bag of sweets or eleven rupees—ten plus one for good luck. I brought her an embroidered shawl which my mother had hand-picked.

Dhondutai wore a new sari for the occasion. We all sat around the room, gossiping with Ayi, fighting for Dhondutai's attention, commenting on the price of potatoes that season. Jane sat in one corner, smiling blithely at the rest, quite content not to understand any of the chatter.

'Ayi, you are looking so well,' said Kuntatai. 'I know you are going to live ten more years.' The old lady smiled back at her, hitting her head softly with her hand, as if to say, arre baba, who wants to live that long!

'Baiji, this is delicious,' said Mandy, picking up the last sweet on the tray.

'A great artiste on stage will be a great artiste everywhere, even in the kitchen,' explained Kuntatai solemnly. She then turned to Jane and said, in hesitant English, 'She is geeneeyus, no?'

'She means, Dhondutai is a genius,' I piped up.

'Of course,' said Jane softly. 'She is glorious. She is the ultimate guru.'

The women nodded.

Dhondutai pretended she didn't care about the gifts. But after everyone had left, she and I joked about each one, while munching on the chocolates. She let me pull open the gift wrappings, making sure I didn't tear them so that she could stash away the pretty papers.

'What does Mandy think, that I am a young bride or something?' she laughed, opening up the bright silk sari. 'I'll keep it aside for you, for when you get married. And these chocolates? I think I prefer our local Amul, not these London ones, no?' We both laughed.

'Enough joking. You must learn something new today. It is an auspicious day.'

I had scarcely begun to understand the significance of a 'guru' in my life. My teachers at school were mostly underpaid, disgruntled players in an education system which emphasized book learning rather than original thinking. Most of them had been gradually numbed by textbooks, testing methods, and disinterested students who often relied on dubious methods—including bribing a clerk to get the exam papers—to get by. There were some memorable teachers who took their role seriously, but most hardly aspired to such lofty pretensions.

When a teacher walked into a classroom, we were trained to jump up and greet them, but this show of respect had nothing to do with how we really felt. Rather, there was mutual disdain. The teachers viewed students as incorrigible brats who knew they could get by in life regardless of whether they understood the beauty of Byron. And we looked upon our mentors as boring old drones with funny regional accents.

The medieval poet, Kabir, extolled the importance of a teacher in one of his many pithy verses: Guru, Govind, dono khade, ka ko laagu paye/ Balihari guru apne Govind diyo dikhaye. If both my teacher and God are standing in front of me, who should I bow before first? The obvious answer would be God. But Kabir suggested that it should be the teacher, for it was he or she who showed the way to God… and wisdom. The teacher in traditional India was considered an avatar of God. The Urdu word taleem, which broadly describes the teaching process, literally translates into 'a glimpse of the universe'.

But somewhere along the way, the revered guru had been replaced by a Dickensian headmaster. The only place where a guru was still regarded with unconditional respect was in the traditional arts.

To extract the best from a teacher, the student had to first prove his complete loyalty and devotion. Some ran away from home to learn, others showed their commitment by running little errands for their guru—massaging his feet, fetching his opium pipe, cooking his meals, tolerating his eccentricities. There is a story about a Hindu singer who was a strict vegetarian, but when his Muslim ustad asked him to cook his favorite dish, he swallowed a life-long revulsion to meat and conjured up a mouth-watering lamb curry.

Teachers, in turn, were not always very god-like. Indeed, many tended to be whimsical, unpredictable, even exploitative. The flautist Hariprasad Chaurasia has described how he spent years begging Annapurna Devi to take him on as a student. Finally, two years later, she agreed, but on the condition that he be prepared to unlearn everything he had ever learned and start from scratch. To do this, he was forced to change his playing position from the right hand to the left.

It was only when a teacher found his student suitably sincere, that he began sharing the secrets of his knowledge. This is why students were encouraged to live with their teachers for a length of time and imbibe every thing about their lives and their art. The spaces between the teaching of music were as important as the teaching itself.

The teacher did not always expect money or material compensation. But there was an unwritten rule that the student would never betray his teacher, especially musically. For the student now carried the guru's name on his lapel; he was his messenger for posterity and represented his style and tutelage.

Today, there is a great deal of debate over why the teaching of Indian music cannot be transposed into a western-style conservatory system which is not subject to the whims of any one teacher. In fact, a number of universities have tried to incorporate the ideas of classroom and curriculum into musical scholarship. But most have failed to turn out inspired musicians. It remains a world bound in mystifying tradition and irrational obsession.

Dhondutai did not expect me to be obsequious. She was remarkably progressive without even knowing it. Yet, she believed that, in this age of multiple distractions, the best way to learn music was through a gurukul, where students lived with the teacher—not because they would be available to massage her feet and make her morning tea, but because to learn this music they had to eat, drink and breathe it all the time. That was the only way. When one student was being taught, the others should sit by and listen, pick up on the mistakes and the corrections, memorize the composition. Yet, the teacher had to establish a rapport with each student individually, to bring forth his or her distinguishing quality.

Dhondutai dreamed not of riches or fame, but of a sparkling white cottage that would sit among emerald-green fields, of a place where she would lovingly distribute the gems of the Jaipur school of music among numerous worthy and eager disciples. Here, music could go back to what it once was—a medium for the divine. She fantasized about it endlessly. Maybe it could be built in Kolhapur, where this music had once reached its zenith. Or it could be somewhere in the outskirts of Bombay, not too far from a train station so that people could come and go easily. She debated the various options in her head. However, her plan remained a dream.

Seven

There is a story about the legendary singer Ustad Alladiya Khan that makes its way around the music world in India.

As long as he breathed, he sang. At the crack of dawn, the Khansahib would start on the lowest octave and the notes would emerge like a Gregorian chant. As the sun rose over the sleepy town of Kolhapur, he gradually built up to the higher notes. The music drifted out of the green stained glass windows of his home. When his voice had blended into the sounds of the day, he sang a morning raga for a couple of hours, until his students started trickling in.

After an afternoon nap, Alladiya Khan took his evening walk around the local lake. If a tall, bespectacled man in loose pajamas, a stiff coat and a pale pink turban, twirling a walking cane while humming to himself, didn't show up one evening, the entire town would buzz with concern. Finally, after dinner, the master once again picked up his instrument and practiced a raga dedicated to the night. If his grandchildren were around him, and he was in a playful mood, he sang a lighter melody.

One evening, a young writer on his way to an all-night music theatre, passed the maestro's house after dinner and heard him practising a particularly complicated taan—a piece that shot up, did a number of stunning trapeze swings, and twirled its way down a spiral, all in one breath. He did it over and over, but one note kept slipping. The writer listened for a while under the window, dragging on a clove cigarette, and then went his way. It was close to four in the morning when the writer, intoxicated with music and sleeplessness, staggered back. When he passed by the great singer's window, he heard him practising the same taan. It was now perfect.

The day Dhondutai told me this story, I was chewing gum. I slowed down my pace in deference to the tale, as she unraveled it softly, while strumming the tanpura. My thirteen-year-old mind may not have absorbed the gravity of the anecdote, but I was mature enough to realize its significance, to understand that it was about the pursuit of excellence. Of course, I would die before revealing that to her.

'It sounds like he was a bored old man, baiji… ' I said insolently, not meaning a word of what I said.

'You know, you are a foolish child. You just do not understand the meaning of discipline. That is why, despite having all the resources in the world, and this God-gifted voice, you are a waste. Forget singing, you won't succeed in anything… '

Years later, I would pine for that moment. I would wish that she had been even harsher with me, perhaps asked me to get out of her house for being so disrespectful of the Khansahib, of this music, and of her. I would regret that I had grown up taking every thing for granted—suddenly it would all be gone, and all I would have with me would be some old photographs and half-forgotten ragas.

Instead, she softened up and said, 'The reason I get angry is, I just want you to learn. You know how it is; there are only two kinds of people who can really devote themselves unconditionally to this art: an amir or a fakir—someone who is rich and doesn't need to worry about making a living, or someone who is too poor to care.'

I was her only hope. The scriptures on music say that there are five types of musicians—the entertainer, the academic, the imitator, the emotional singer. The fifth is a teacher. Dhondutai knew that even if she never became a big name herself, she could be the king-maker. She wanted me to be her little Bhairavi, who would take this music forward. It must not die with her.

Eight

Sometimes, my mother accompanied me to my music lessons, stepping over the dirt puddles and ignoring the pimps who scratched their testicles and whispered obscenities on the street. 'Oye memsahib, zara dekh ke chalo,' one had hissed at her as she walked into Congress House. Few mothers I knew would have allowed their young daughters to step into such dubious terrain, but we were an adventurous pair.

The days she visited, Dhondutai and I would together present our achievements to the audience of two doting mothers—hers would continue to stare at the wall, and mine would be visibly moved by my growing prowess as a classical singer.

The years that I had blindly followed my teacher's instructions, doing endless scales and learning how to spiral up and down with crackling speed, were now bearing fruit. I too began to enjoy hearing myself do things that were considered extraordinary. I could now sing two or three different ragas—not just the scales, but the way they were performed. That meant, starting with the verse, moving into the gradual aalaap which builds up to a faster pace and then my favorite part, the superfast taans where I could really display my virtuosity. Dhondutai had taught me how to take a deep breath to get a head start and then spin out a nimble taan which gyrated up and down like a Russian gymnast on a pommel horse.

In the middle of the lesson, especially when my mother was in attendance, Dhondutai sometimes stopped teaching and started singing. It happened seamlessly, where she moved from instruction to performance. It was a part of the training, for we learn as much just from listening. I continued playing the tanpura while she carried on, spurred by my mother's sighs of appreciation.

These were some of her most beautiful moments as a musician. She sang with abandon. She was not on stage, trying to prove a point to some semi-literate music critic or rival artiste who may or may not have been there. She took the little leaps and risks that can only be taken when one lets go, when there is nothing at stake but the magic of the moment.

'That was so beautiful, baiji,' my mother said once, when Dhondutai finished a long movement in Raga Tilak Kamod. 'I almost preferred this singing to the time you sang this in the Matunga concert. I don't know what it was. It felt lighter and more free.'

Dhondutai dismissed my mother's comment with a good-natured laugh and went back to teaching me. We had a very fruitful lesson and we were all in a very good mood when we left.

One afternoon, my mother came to pick me up, but arrived a little early. She looked pensive as she sat on her usual place on the bed. She leaned forward, resting her head in her hands, and watched me intently with that embarrassing you-are-the-best-child-in-the-whole-world stare that could pierce a hole through your head. I started singing—what else?—Raga Bhoop. But right in the middle of a magnificent taan, which climbed up, three notes at a time, I suddenly started coughing uncontrollably.

I had been suffering from a recurring cough for several weeks. It would come and go, sometimes with a low fever. Our family physician, the good Dr Bhatt, had not been able to diagnose it and blamed Bombay's winter pollution, when the fog descended and did not let up. But it had my parents understandably worried. Even Dhondutai had been a bit concerned because it interrupted my singing lessons.

Dhondutai waited patiently for my cough to settle, and rummaged in her purse for a little vial which contained some ayurvedic throat lozenges. Suddenly, I saw my mother holding her face in her hands and sobbing. I stared at her in fear and embarassed disbelief. Dhondutai put her purse down and quietly got up to comfort her.

'Baiji... I don't know what to do. This cough doesn't seem to go and the doctor has not been able to diagnose it. You know, our cook has just been treated for a mild case of tuberculosis. What if... ' My mother gathered herself as Dhondutai sat next to her, and dabbed her cheeks gently with the end of her sari.

'Don't worry. I have been wanting to talk to you about this for a while,' she said, soothingly. 'I will take care of it, but you will have to follow my instructions without questioning me. You see, the thing is, someone has cast an evil eye on your daughter. And I suspect it could be after that concert in Matunga.'

My mother silently nodded and wiped her eyes. Dhondutai continued, 'But these things can be reverted. Here's what I will need... ' She rattled off a list of things—a coconut, a garland of marigolds, two incense sticks, and three yards of sacred thread.

During my next lesson, I was made to sit on the sofa with the marigold garland around my neck, looking like a horrendous child goddess, while my teacher circulated a hairy brown coconut around my head three times, muttering a mantra. I was deeply embarrassed. Bhakti Maya had shut her eyes and folded her hands in deference. My mother also shut her eyes, evidently adding her own bit to the force of prayer. She was instructed to take the flowers and the fruit and throw them into the ocean, for they carried with them the bad spirit that had settled inside me to prevent me from continuing my training with Dhondutai.

For seven days after that, Dhondutai prayed to the goddess, and kept a glass of water in front of her. The days I went to her, she would make me drink the water. On the days I wasn't there, she poured the water into the small basil plant that sat nestled in her kitchen window.

I don't know whether it was the coconut ritual, the plant, or a heavy dose of vitamins, but my cough disappeared.

Dhondutai's world was filled with superstition and paranoia, which is common to people in the performing arts. She believed in spirits that existed beyond the realm of human perception and was convinced that they were always at work, either protecting or disabling, depending on where (or who) they came from. She wore a solitary black bangle on her right wrist which she said absorbed and deflected any evil vibration that was being sent her way. She carried her own flask of tea when she went to a concert because—who knows?—there might have been that jealous singer or organizer who would spike her beverage. Why take chances when you could prevent such things? She was a fierce believer in stars and their signs, and linked colors to days of the week, which in turn connected to different astral planes. She picked the color of her sari based on that—if it was Saturday, it had to be blue—and made sure that she never wore the 'enemy' color that day, like I had once done.

I always scoffed at her beliefs, which found no place in my rational frame of reference. It took me a long time to realize that one could not—and must not—question faith. Each of us has our own way of making a pact with life.

Dhondutai gave me a mantra, a single line, which she said I should recite whenever I could, as many times as possible during the day. She said the goddess would always protect me.

Many years later, Dhondutai told me the story of how she was practicing early one morning and saw the vision of the goddess while she sang Raga Bhairavi. 'You may laugh at me if you want, but it did happen. And this was not the first time. It has happened to Alladiya Khan and to many musicians whom the gods have chosen to bless.'

I didn't laugh. I had begun to realize, in the smallest way, that this music had celestial roots and that those who had entered its folds and drunk its notes, generally floated a few inches above the mortal universe.

Part II
Shivaji Park

One

I was fourteen when Ayi died.

Bhakti Maya gave me the news, tears rolling down her cheeks. I wasn't home when Dhondutai called to cancel the lesson. She spoke to Bhakti and told her that she had to rush to Jabalpur, to her sister. Ayi had been visiting her younger daughter Shakuntala when she passed away in her sleep. She had muttered Dhondutai's name before she lay down and closed her eyes.

Dhondutai was still mourning in Jabalpur when she got the news about Mausi's massive heart attack. The expert nurse who had pumped life into so many others, was not able to do anything for herself when her body succumbed, with an exhausted gasp, to a lifetime of troubles. She was alone in the apartment when it happened. The neighbours broke into the flat after the cleaning woman banged on their door and said that Mausi was not answering her bell. Mausi's children decided to sell the flat, which they knew would get them a good price. The neighbourhood was being gradually gentrified. There were fewer takers for the traditional dance parlors. Most of the working women had moved out and trained their daughters to dance in the more profitable, strobe-lit ladies' bars in the suburbs. Besides, Kennedy Bridge was in the heart of midtown, where space was equivalent to gold.

Dhondutai returned from Jabalpur, alone for the first time in her life. She was also soon going to be homeless. She did not want to move in with her brother and his family in Delhi. She loved them dearly, but the city's air pollution would surely destroy her voice—or, at least, that was the excuse she gave her family. The truth is, she valued her independence. She loved the city by the sea. Bombay welcomed lonely fringe elements like her and humoured them without judgment.

I received a message that Dhondutai had called while I was vacationing with my family in the hills. I did not imagine what she was going through, left alone twice-over in the small flat in Congress House. She started teaching right away. From then on, her students would be the only source of human companionship that would come her way.

Her longtime student, Manjutai, whom she had taught on and off over the years, invited her to come and stay with her in her sprawling house in Shivaji Park, until she found a new home. Dhondutai never liked taking favours from anyone, but Manjutai and her kind husband, Dada, insisted. They called her over for lunch one day and broached the subject.

'Tai, don't even think twice about it. After all, we have such a large house, and now that Madhu is married and gone, there are only the two of us.' Manjutai said. She hurriedly added, 'I have my own selfish reasons. This will force me to sit down and have lessons more regularly and we will be privileged to have music constantly resound in the house.'

Dhondutai felt more comfortable once this equation was established. If she taught Manjutai every day, she would not feel such a weight of obligation. This would be her form of payback. She also knew that she didn't have much choice at this point.

'What about my students?'

'You can freely carry on with your lessons as well,' Manjutai assured.

'And meals?'

'You will eat with us, of course, tai. You are free to use the kitchen, but you know quite well that Ramu and Ratan will be honored to cook for you just as they do for us.'

Dada gently added, 'Tai, believe me, you would be doing us a favor by staying here. If you are around, Manju and I can travel abroad together for longer stretches, and not be concerned about one of us rushing back to take care of things in the house.'

Dhondutai felt a burden lifting from her shoulders. She despised the chores of cutting vegetables and cleaning, which ate into her music time. This would really be a relief.

'Manjutai, thank you for helping me. I really appreciate it. Let me think about it.'

But it must be a temporary arrangement, she told herself. She would have to do something about finding her own place. She decided that it was time to step out of her seclusion and get in touch with one of those wretched government officers for some help.

The state government's department of culture routinely allots apartments to certain groups—such as journalists, scholars, artistes and scientists—at cost price. There were long lists of applicants awaiting approval, many of whom were undeserving. But corruption was the norm and it didn't take much imagination to push an application through. Over the years, numerous less accomplished musicians had extracted this privilege and been given flats in the new housing colonies that were sprouting up all over the city. Many of these musicians subsequently sold them at a profit and moved back into their old homes, crowded with tablas and sitars and nieces and nephews. Dhondutai decided to send in an application for a flat under the 'performing artiste' quota. She knew, however, that she would have to find someone to push this through for her.

She called on the only person she knew with some clout—the nephew of her teacher, Kesarbai. He happened to be a successful executive. He would do anything for any one connected to his aunt. Mr Kerkar immediately put in a call to the government officer concerned, and Dhondutai's application magically moved to the top of the pile.

Mausi's daughter gently informed Dhondutai that she could stay in the flat until she found alternate accommodation, but that they had found a buyer at a good price and he was anxious to get on with the transaction. If there was one thing Dhondutai cherished, it was her pride. She would not be a liability on any one. By the end of the month, she would leave Kennedy Bridge and its flickering fairy lights for ever. She started to plan her departure.

One afternoon, a few weeks later, after picking up vegetables from her usual stall down the road, she went to see the recycling vendor. His small shop was crowded with objects that had once held their own but had been discarded, like aging mistresses, to make way for a new order. They were the detritus of daily living—like the enormous brass kettle, which once had bubbled and churned out nourishing cups of tea for an entire village but had become a misfit in a small city kitchen; or the mouldy stacks of twenty-year-old *National Geographic*s which had been painstakingly preserved until their subscriber died and his grandchildren had no room for Masai warriors and warbling whales. Rows of empty scotch bottles with their labels intact waited to be refilled, resealed, and resold to some unsuspecting drunk.

Dhondutai asked the shopkeeper to stop by her flat on the third floor. He said he would send his man in an hour. She walked slowly up the stairs of Congress House, opened the latch key, and went straight to her room. She placed the small bag of vegetables on the blue coffee table and sat down on her sofa-bed. For a few minutes, she stared listlessly at the empty bed along the wall. But before her eyes started blurring, she quickly checked herself and started organizing her things. Later that morning, the recycling man came in and took away the bed and the wooden chair with the portable toilet. Mementos of a life, sold for two hundred rupees.

There was only one way to comfort herself. She picked up the tanpura. She sang Raga Sukhiya Bilawal because it was an afternoon raga and it was nearing that time of day. 'Oh you, Devi Durga, who protects the good sages, take care of me.' The door bell rang. She put down the tanpura and got up. It was the postman.

'Namaskar tai. You have a registered letter.' He grinned at her. 'Can I get a glass of water?'

'Sure. But you'd better bring me good tidings in return for this,' she laughed. She went inside and looked at the envelope. It was from the state department of arts and culture.

She shut the door, turned the latch, and walked slowly to the kitchen where she slit open the envelope with a knife.

It was a letter telling her she had been allotted a two-bedroom flat in Borivli, but would need to put down fifty thousand rupees within two months.

Dhondutai sat down on her bed, her head spinning. Where would she get that much? Half that amount was no problem—her brother had told her he would arrange for that much. But the rest? She only had about fifteen thousand on her. Her heart sank when she realized what she might have to do. She opened the innermost chamber of her cupboard and took two gold bangles out. They had been given to her mother by the queen of Kolhapur when Dhondutai was a little girl. The beautifully filigreed pieces gleamed in her hand, reminding her of a childhood lost, mocking the success she had not achieved in adulthood. How could she possibly sell these? She turned them around her fingers. The patterns on them were reminiscent of the flowers that grew along the lake in Kolhapur. Her eyes once again started to fill up. Stop it, she told herself. You have to be practical, not emotional. She put the bangles back and resolved to take them to the jeweller. Perhaps she could buy them back when she had the money.

The day I returned to Mumbai, I went straight to Congress House. I saw Ayi's toilet chair was missing and felt a strange sensation in the pit of my stomach and my eyes well up. I was confused by the feeling and tried to deflect it. But the little room was filled with a painful absence.

My mother came to pick me up from the lesson, and to offer her condolences for Ayi's passing on. She had no idea that Dhondutai would also be moving soon. Dhondutai told her about the government flat that had been offered to her.

'I am running short of about fifteen thousand rupees, and was planning to sell my gold to raise that amount.

Maybe you could think about buying them, they're so beautiful, and I would be happy if they went to a good family. After all, Namita would get to wear them.' She took them out and showed them to my mother.

'Don't even think about selling these,' protested my mother. 'You will get the price of the gold, but what about this stunning workmanship! No one is going to pay you for that. You don't have to worry about the money. We will lend it to you. You can pay us back whenever you can.'

'Are you sure, Meeraji? Do you want to ask Namita's father first?'

'There won't be a problem. You must absolutely not sell them.'

The bangles remained with Dhondutai. As soon as she had a concert, she paid my mother back.

On the last day of the month, she moved into Manjutai's spacious, welcoming house. Shivaji Park was a tree-lined neighbourhood that had come up around a large green park, in the centre of which was a statue of the famous Maratha warrior king, Shivaji. The area around the park was inhabited by genteel old timers like Manjutai and Dada, who still believed in things like morning walks and evening ragas. In a city where property had long ceased to be what it was once intended to be—a means of accommodation—and had, instead turned into the biggest cause of family feuds, corruption, even murder, this couple had opened their home to someone with no vested interest. They believed that an artiste of Dhondutai's stature deserved to be comfortable, that was all. And they were happy to be in a position where they could help.

The house sprawled over almost half a block. Many years ago, the family had rented the ground floor to a government school. Over the years, the old rent laws saw to it that the school remained, and the family learned to live with the laughter of children as they filed in and out of their backyard. Their lives subconsciously tuned in to the school's timings. The morning bell meant it was time for tea and the newspaper. The closing bell usually signaled the end of lunch, time for a quick nap.

Dhondutai moved into a suite at the far end of a long open corridor on the second floor, which gave her privacy. Hardly anyone went there, not even Tito, Manjutai's attention-seeking Doberman, who made it a point to bound through every room in the house. Her room opened onto a generous-sized balcony from where she could see a sliver of the park. One of the first things she did was to install a tulsi plant.

The tanpuras arrived first and were given pride of place against two beautiful old teak wood cupboards that stood on either side of the room. The rest of the furniture—her prayer altar, the paisley-patterned rug, the blue steel cupboard and, of course, the three pictures on the walls—that had occupied her room in Congress House, also found their place in different corners of the room. They looked resplendent now that they had been taken out of the poky room they had occupied for so many years. But she never uttered a word in comparison. After all, that had been her home.

Shivaji Park was much further away from where I lived and, now that I was fourteen, I could take the public bus or train on my own, without my old ayah or mother in tow. The local train became a new adventure for me, and opened up yet another fascinating, frightening world that was far removed from the cocoon I otherwise occupied.

The trains are Bombay's arteries. They ferry millions of people back and forth every day. If, for some reason, the flow stopped, the city would lapse into a coma. The trains were like mobile homes, with their own unique rules and etiquette which had to be followed, or you were thrown out—literally. Before I embarked on my first train journey to Shivaji Park, I had been told two things about this snaky beast. One, that there were separate compartments for women, and two, that I had to get off at Dadar. But this was hardly enough information, I would soon find out. It was like landing in a foreign country with an outdated tourist brochure.

The first time I took the train, I bought the ticket and stood on the platform, trying to decipher the blinking lights and numbers that announced timings and destinations. Then, I made the cardinal mistake of Bombay train travel. I got on at half past four in the afternoon or, to be more accurate, I tried to get on. It was the most terrifying experience of my life, second only to the time I fell off the somersault horse and displayed my underwear to a hall full of sniggering classmates. Rule number one about the trains is, if you want to travel anywhere during the rush hour, you'd better get on at the very first stop. This is the downstream syndrome. The further away you are from the office district, where the train starts, the greater the force of the human river. The droves pack themselves in at the first stop, and by the second stop, the compartment is a can of sweaty, irritable human sardines. I hadn't the faintest idea that Grant Road station, which is where I was getting on, was stops away from downtown, and that I would be out-maneuvered by a group of oversized vegetable sellers who had been up since five that morning and were determined to make it home.

A few minutes later, I was back at my house, dialling Dhondutai's number.

'Baiji, I couldn't get on the train...'

'Oh, beta. I should have warned you to leave a little earlier. Don't worry. Come tomorrow. And remember, leave no later than four or you'll get caught in the rush.' She was excessively protective of me and was quite touched that I had even attempted to negotiate with this terrifying dragon that zoomed in and out of the city breathing fire, just to get to her.

Over the next month, I started learning the rules. Avoid the busy hours. Don't wait too long for people to get off before getting aboard, align your body with the person in front of you so that you get pushed in automatically. If you don't get a place to sit, start asking those already seated where they are getting off and reserve your place.

I soon became a veteran. I was probably one of the only girls in my ninth grade class who was allowed to take public transport, that too alone. While I could have taken the bus, I preferred the train for two reasons. It was much faster, and I was completely intrigued by the world it opened up. The second-class ladies' compartment was like being inside an afternoon talk show featuring women I would never otherwise meet, and I loved eavesdropping on conversations about wicked mothers-in-law, deadbeat husbands, mean bosses, and the price of rice. Some women spent almost four hours a day on the trains—more time than they would get with their children. They would get into the same compartment, day after day. It was the space in which they developed bonds outside the ones that had been forced on them. This was where they exchanged home remedies and recipes. They mourned for each other but also shared happy stories about their children's school results. The commuter understood why the woman next to her had a bruised arm, and she showed her quiet support by squeezing in so she could get more room on the seat. Anonymity gave them strength.

It was a dazzlingly hot Friday afternoon when I stumbled off a train and wended my way through the crowds into the street that would lead me to Manjutai's house. The street was the site for all the dramas that played out in the city—a perennial battleground for the war between the local government and the roadside vendor whose shop consisted of a makeshift table or rack which paid no heed to licenses and store fronts. This collection of informal vendors made for an open air mall of sorts: brassieres and panties dangled unabashedly like filigreed stalagmites, right next to a leaning tower of stainless steel bowls on one side of the street; gleaming vegetables lay in neat piles on the other side—it was all strategically organized, so that women could do a quick run and stock up on everything at once on their way back from work. Hundreds of vendors had established their place on the street, conducting brisk business with the streams of commuters that went in and out of the station every day. The atmosphere was vaguely medieval.

The street had its own system of order and functioned through unwritten codes. Further down, at the next stop, when the local Muslim population gathered at the mosque on Fridays, the street would make way for the flocks of devotees who kneeled in synchronized submission to the voice of the muezzin that floated out of a loudspeaker.

I haggled with a young woman for a string of jasmine which I wanted to buy for my teacher. She wouldn't budge on her price, and invited me to 'take a whiff'. Packing it deftly in a green leaf, she balanced a sleeping baby in her arms, and handed the jasmine to me with a cheeky grin.

I ambled through the bazaar and crossed the street, passing an ugly building with the face of an angry tiger painted on its front. It was the headquarters of the right-wing Hindu party, Shiv Sena, well-situated for this was a distinctly Hindu middle class neighbourhood. Two blocks further, across the street from a statue covered with pigeon shit, stood Manjutai's house.

At the entrance to the house, I ran into a gaggle of school children marching out in twos for their evening exercise in the park. The shrill bell set Tito off and I heard him barking inside. The cook Ratan opened the door, rubbing his eyes, and trying to hush the dog. When Tito sniffed me, the bark petered down to a welcoming growl.

The house was still covered with a soporific film, but the pot of tea brewing in the kitchen would soon prepare it for the evening bustle. Dhondutai was in the kitchen, getting two cups ready. I handed her the flowers. She thanked me and laughed at the idea of wearing them in her hair, but then did attach them to her little ponytail.

'Mmm. The tea is delicious, baiji,' I said, and got the beam of satisfaction I was looking for.

'Arre, you know when I was your age, we used to drink tea on the sly! Our father never touched tea because it was considered a stimulant. He only drank a glass of warm milk in the morning and evening, and expected his family to do the same. But of course, my grandmother loved tea and that's what got us all hooked on it. Tea was bought along with the other groceries on the pretext that it was meant for the occasional guest. It was hilarious. If our father was home, the teapot would be slung on a rope and dragged up secretly through an opening in the ceiling to the second floor, where we children would be waiting with our glasses.'

'That is so funny, baiji! To think that tea was the drug of your times...'

'We were all so disciplined. My father used to insist that even my teacher Bhurji Khan drink only milk when he came for my lesson. On the days when my father was out, he would peek into the kitchen and sheepishly say to Ayi, "Sonatai, can I please have a cup of tea today?"'

We laughed at the idea of this lion-like man sneaking around to drink his tea, and slurped at our own. While we were bantering, I noticed a gorgeous young woman standing half-hidden behind a door between the kitchen and a small inner room. She was wearing a moss-green traditional Maharashtrian nine-yard sari, and her hand was covered with glass bangles, a darker shade of green. She smiled shyly at me. I raised my eyebrows questioningly at my teacher and she explained that the girl was Ratan's young bride who had just come from the village. She would stay there for a few months before he took her back. This was Manjutai's home—open to everyone.

We walked through the long corridor to get to Dhondutai's room at the far end. I kept pace with her as she shuffled along in her flip-flops, complaining about the oppressive weather, while Tito ran to and fro, racing ahead and then back to us, unable to slow down to Dhondutai's deliberate rhythm. As we passed the living room, I glanced into one of the rooms and waved to Manjutai who was sipping tea while going over the dinner menu with Ramu the cook. She peered over her bifocals and waved back.

Dhondutai's room was cooler than the rest of the house because it was shaded by two splendid gulmohar trees which periodically sent wispy crimson petals floating into the house. She reached for the tanpura, revealing a wet half-moon under her sleeve, and pulled it out of its faded pink and gold cover in the familiar motion—untying the knot at its head and scrolling the cloth off the sleeve. She cringed as she played it. It was badly out of tune. The heat and humidity had caused the wood to swell up and the four taut strings had lost their moorings. She began to turn the tuning knob slowly and it creaked back in resistance like an obdurate child.

Dhondutai stopped tuning midway and said, 'I think it's time for you to learn how to do this yourself. This will be your companion for life, so you may as well learn how to make it work for you.' She handed over the instrument to me as one would a small baby.

Many years later, after my son was born, she would tell me, 'Remember, look after the tanpura with the same care as you would your son, Chaitanya.'

'The tanpura is not an inanimate thing, you know. There is life in it. It responds to swara just like the human ear. You may not believe this, but I have experienced this with my own eyes. I would not have believed it...' Dhondutai lapsed into a story about one of the times she accompanied Kesarbai on stage.

She had just started learning with Kesarbai. She'd heard stories about her teacher's temper when performing in public and was a little nervous about sitting behind her. The concert was scheduled for six that evening. The musicians came on, carrying their instruments, and sat on the stage—first Dhondutai, with the tanpura, then the tabla player and the sarangi player. Finally, the much-awaited Kesarbai came on, in her trademark white silk sari. The accompanists began tuning their instruments—the sarangi player picked up his bow and moved it across the strings lovingly, playing a slow sa to help the tanpura get the correct pitch. The tabaliya was also tinkering around with his tabla, getting it to tune. In her nervousness, Dhondutai wasn't able to get the instrument to sound just right. A few minutes later, Kesarbai looked at her wrist watch, frowned and turned to her accompanists, oblivious that she was speaking into the microphone, 'What's wrong with you people? You can't get something so simple? I can't wait till tomorrow.' And, while they sat there, paralyzed with fear, she lifted one hand to her ear and belted out a brilliant sa.

'It was miraculous,' said Dhondutai. 'The minute she sang the note, both the tanpura and the tabla just fell into tune by themselves. It was as if the power of her perfect pitch reached the very core of the instruments and they responded.'

I looked at Dhondutai, incredulous. But I had long learned not to argue with her on matters that were beyond the realm of my imagination. I simply responded with a soft 'Wo!'

A musician's accompaniments are her companions for life. As Dhondutai said, 'Spouses die. Children move on. Even your own faculties start failing you as you get older. But these will stay with you for ever, if you look after them.'

That day, she decided that it was time for me to get my own tanpura. She would write to Abba in Miraj, the town known for its hereditary instrument craftsmen. Abba's family had made musical instruments for generations, seasoning the wood for a year, polishing it down, painstakingly inlaying bits of ivory into the borders. Their work was a labour of love and they did it because it was all they knew. But it no longer fed the family, for most younger musicians were gravitating towards the more convenient and portable electronic tanpuras and tablas.

Dhondutai clutched her handbag as we clambered into the second class ladies' compartment. Despite the chaotic flow of people in and out, she waited for me to board before she did. She spent the entire train ride with her handkerchief held against her nose, to fend off the stench from the fresh fish being carried by three fisherwomen. No one dared to say anything to the fierce looking women for they risked having a wide-eyed pomfret dangled in front of their nose.

We were on our way to a music instrument shop. Dhondutai had written to Abba, describing the kind of tanpura she wanted for me. It was to be exactly like the pair he had made for her. They were an amalgamation of the designs on her two teachers' instruments. The intricately patterned paisleys were taken from Kesarbai's tanpura, the spiral border from Bhurji Khan's instrument. She had designed her tanpuras as a tribute to both gurus.

But it would be a while before Abba delivered. She knew it could take upto a year before he would send them across from Miraj, So we were headed to a store to get interim relief in the form of a plug-and-play tanpura, a neat little electronic box which simulated the drone of the real thing.

I needed this to practice at home because I was to make my first solo public appearance soon, at my school's annual music talent competition.

Dhondutai had decided to teach me Raga Malhar, for it was nearing that time of the year when the scorching heat would give way to a heady monsoon. Malhar is the raga of the rain. Its uplifting melodic phrases sing of replenishment and rebirth. I was first introduced to Malhar through a story in *Amar Chitra Katha*. It was about Tansen. A rival of the great musician plotted to kill him. His weapon was music. He urged the king to make Tansen sing the powerful Raga Deepak, whose notes supposedly generate heat. As Tansen sang, the lights in the palace miraculously came on.

His singing became so intense that his temperature shot up and he was consumed with a fever. This was when his daughter picked up the tanpura and sang Raga Malhar, to cool things down. Tansen was saved!

Bhauji's shop for musical instruments was in a small lane off Lamington Road, close to Dhondutai's old home in Congress House. We stopped for a second to examine the shop window. It displayed a sitar, a tabla set, two guitars, and a keyboard, proclaiming its entry into a more western music era. As we walked in, we were assailed by the scent of wood and varnish. Rows and rows of tablas and their percussive cousins, the dholaks, lined one shelf; a band of harmoniums perched on one another. Tanpuras and sitars of all shapes and sizes, with gleaming gourds, some patterned, some stark and bare-bottomed, hung like sculptures from the walls. Numerous other instruments lay strewn about.

A pock-faced man behind the counter put down his glass of tea and looked at us without much enthusiasm. I leaned against the counter and cringed when my arm touched a sticky circle where the glass had earlier been placed.

'Namaskar. I am Dhondutai Kulkarni. Is Bhauji around?' Dhondutai was always quaintly formal and old-fashioned in her interactions.

The man stared at her, almost through her. Then, he took a noisy slurp from his glass and said that this shop had been sold two years ago to one Bachubhai. He had no idea where we could find Bhauji. 'What are you looking for?'

'We would like an electronic tanpura, please.'

The salesman produced two models. She picked one, I paid for it, and we left.

Dhondutai was very quiet on the way home. I didn't question her, but I instinctively knew why she was silent. I began to realize why she rarely went out. It was true that she didn't care for superfluous socializing, but there was also a part of her that didn't want to run into the painful reality of anonymity. She might have been a serious musician, the only disciple of one of the greatest singers of all time, the repository of an enviable collection of rare ragas and compositions, but the world didn't care. It was attuned to a different sound. This was one of those encounters that reminded her that she was alone, striving to find a voice in a universe that paid less and less attention to someone who had not quite achieved that rare balance between great art and public recognition.

I started to prep for the school music competition. I had lived in two worlds since the day I had begun my singing lessons. When I was at school, I hid the fact that I regularly visited a place called Shivaji Park, often in crowded trains or lumbering red buses, to learn music. When I was with Dhondutai, I refrained from telling her that girls my age had boyfriends or that I had taken my first drag from a cigarette. It was impossible to mix the two spaces. But one of the few times they overlapped was when I participated in the music competition.

My school was based on the English public school system. It was about fierce competition and rigid class hierarchies. Besides the academic curriculum, school life was divided into four 'houses'—red, blue, green and yellow, named after long-dead, hoary British headmasters. I belonged to the morbidly named 'Savage' house, which was green. Each house was stratified into an intricate ladder of house captains and monitors whose mission was to ensure that their color racked up the most points at the end of the year. So, our school lives were essentially divided into a series of 'inter-house' competitions. Red competed with blue in the boxing ring, and articulate teams of Savages debated against equally well-trained Palmer-ites on subjects like 'do joint families work better than nuclear families' or 'arranged marriage versus love unions.' When the inter-house music competition rolled around, I offered my humble services and said I would participate in the 'Indian vocal' category.

It was when I was being trained for my first little performance on this indifferent platform that I was first introduced to the concepts of rhythm and time in music. The person who handled this department in Dhondutai's universe was called Sridhar Padhye, a contemplative man with unnaturally jet black hair who wore white polyester kurtas, nursed a wad of tobacco in his cheek, and played his tabla with his eyes shut. He resembled a sleeping turtle, except when he broke into facial contortions and jerked his elbows while trying to reach his rhythmic climax.

Tuesday was the one day Dhondutai did not teach. Instead, she spent a couple of hours rehearsing, accompanied by Padhye Master. Before they got down to their music business, they would exchange notes on the alignment of the stars and Padhye Master would tell her what lay in store for her over the coming week. After tabla, astrology was his second love. He thrived on reading horoscopes and dodging—or harnessing—the unseen forces that control human destiny. He took himself extremely seriously, and had, of late, extended his interest to numerology, dissecting people's names to tell them whether they would have financial troubles, how soon they would have a child, or when a sickness would go away. His services were gratis.

A few months before my music competition, Dhondutai requested Padhye Master to come once a week in the evening, so that he could accompany me and get me tuned into the extraordinarily meticulous mathematical patterns that share the stage with melody. She had been preparing me for the rhythm section, and taught me to count the beats with my left hand, while I played the tanpura with the right one. The most common cycle used is the sixteen-beat cycle, called teentaal or tritaal. Dha dhin dhin dha. Dha dhin dhin dha. Ta tin tin ta. Ta dhin dhin dha... sixteen beats divided neatly into four times four. The sixteen-beat cycle starts and ends and starts and ends, creating a repetitive circularity; the melody has to accommodate itself within its scaffolding; it has to negotiate with the parameters to find a happy balance between freedom and responsibility, rights and duties, exhilaration and restraint. There is scope for risk-taking, within reason, as long as one came back to the line of control in time, and hit sama, the drum stroke where one cycle ended and the new one began; a point of arrival and of departure. This is a musical metaphor for life as it should be lived. Truly great musicians can swerve into unchartered bylanes, but still find their way back to the destination. On time.

When Padhye Master sat down on my right side, which is where a tabla accompanist always sits, the first thing he said to me, with great aplomb and in English, was, 'notes plus rhythm equals music.' Then, without much ado, he shut his eyes and started playing. That was the only sentence he uttered that day.

Dhondutai guided him on the beat and tempo. Before we started, she said, 'Our scriptures say, sruti mata, laya pita...' which means that the notes are the mother and tempo is the father. 'Now I don't know which is male and which is female,' she added with a laugh, 'but I think the ancient gurus were trying to tell us that the temporal structure of Indian music resonates beautifully with nature.' She explained how every thing in life—both within ourselves and in the outside world—revolves around a circular recurring rhythm. 'Our breathing, one's daily routine, the seasons, the motions of the universe... all follow this pattern. Life is what finds its way in between all these cycles, and that is exactly what music is. It is the ability to live life in conjunction with these patterns and parameters. It is a difficult equilibrium to maintain, but that is where the musician's skill comes in. And our gharana is known for this magnificent coordination between melody and rhythm, where both play off each other, to create a complex, scintillating story.'

Padhye's eyes remained shut through this philosophical interlude. Suddenly, his body contorted, his shoulders shook, he screwed up his eyes, and started limbering up on his instrument. He showcased himself for two minutes, and when he reached the sama, he opened his eyes in time to see our appreciation.

Dhondutai duly responded with a 'wah.' Music is a great deal about performance. One of India's best tabla players, the startlingly handsome Zakir Hussain, performs like a rock star. He draws attention to himself with emotive motions and dramatic gestures. His audience loves him.

For me, it was a challenge just to make it to the sama in time. It is here that you reach a moment of energy in the composition and repeat the melodic refrain. I was taught to recognize the sound of a particular beat, the thirteenth one in the cycle, which would inform me that it was time to wrap up the movement and prepare for the sama. The key, however, is to surprise the listener by reaching it with a flourish, so that the audience gasps in suspense as you land just in time.

'Every time you reach the sama, you must elicit a response from the audience for the movement you have just successfully completed,' said Dhondutai. 'This was Kesarbai's specialty. She didn't just arrive at the sama, but landed majestically, carrying her audience with her.'

The music I had been taught took on another dimension. It became difficult, more interesting, as I learned to work within the mathematical frameworks laid out by the rhythm component. I had to concentrate, for if I missed the sama, I would have to fill in a whole other cycle before I could safely land at the point where the circle stopped and started.

To start with, Dhondutai spoon-fed me, and taught me movements that fit perfectly into the cycle, leaving me no scope to improvise or make mistakes. I would learn six slow movements and six fast ones. Each one tackled new aspects of the raga and its notes. There should be variety in what you present—the audience must not get bored. Four or five lessons later, I was able to present a well manicured, ten-minute performance. Three minutes went in the composition, three minutes of slow aalaap, and two-three minutes of fast taans.

Naturally, I won. No one else in school had been through the rigour of training that I had survived for the last few years. For the next couple of years, even though my seniors didn't remotely understand my music, I became the winning token who would bring points to the house. I was thrust into this unglamorous category, and expected to perform.

Winning first prize didn't make any difference to my status in the school star system, however. Quite the opposite, actually, for it made me stick out as someone who was curiously native and different. After I finished my little rendition, two boys from my class came up to me and said, 'Heh heh! Did you forget the words?' I laughed along with them, not revealing my hurt feelings, and my life continued to be a painful counter-narrative to the lives of other teenagers my age. But after my success at school, Dhondutai looked upon me with even greater adoration.

Two

I was over an hour into my lesson, but was having difficulty with Raga Tilak Kamod. The notes kept slipping into Raga Desh, because they are such close cousins and share common features. I would start out fine, and then suddenly catch myself singing a phrase from Desh. Exasperated, I asked Dhondutai, 'Raga! Gharana! Why does all this matter, as long as it sounds good?'

Dhondutai stopped singing and said softly, 'Because this is the sacred music of Swami Haridas. You cannot tamper with it. Let me tell you a little story... ' She put down her tanpura and motioned to the tabaliya to stop playing. 'Alladiya Khan was actually a Hindu Brahmin.'

I looked at her in amazement. To thus rewrite the history around the founder of the Jaipur Gharana was blasphemy. But Dhondutai didn't look like she was fibbing. She unraveled the story for me.

Alladiya Khan was born into the family of Nath Vishwambhara, the direct descendant of Haridas Swami, the great singer and saint who taught Tansen.

The Nath Vishwambharas were high priests in the royal courts. One of the Khansahib's forefathers was the court musician and head priest of a small princely state called Anup Shahar near Delhi. During a spate of territorial takeovers, the king of Anup Shahar was captured by the emperor of Delhi.

Shortly after the king was taken in, Anup Shahar's court musician disappeared, without telling anyone where he was going. He made his way to the outskirts of Delhi, established himself in a small inn, and started singing. By and by, many gathered to hear him, until the news of his musical genius reached the emperor. The emperor summoned him to his court and asked him to perform. Moved by his music, he said, 'Ask for anything and it will be yours.'

'Anything? Are you sure, sire?' he asked, with a smile.

Expecting the usual request for jewels or property, the emperor nodded nonchalantly.

The canny musician then asked for the release of his king.

Taken aback, the emperor thought for a bit, then said, 'I will release him, but only if you convert to Islam.' The emperor thought that this condition would never be fulfilled by the singer, for faith was the most important thing to man. But in those days, loyalty to the king, who was considered an incarnation of God, superceded all else. Without hesitating, the singer agreed to the condition.

And that is how Alladiya Khan's forefather became a Muslim.

Centuries later, when Alladiya Khan told this story to his biographer, Govindrao Tembe, the scholar asked him, 'Why doesn't your family convert back?'

'Is it necessary?' the Khansahib asked, quietly. 'Besides, even if we convert, will you give us your daughters in marriage? Will you eat bread with us?' Tembe and the assembly of Brahmin scholars who were seated around him were silent. 'If I convert back to Hinduism, I will be neither here nor there. Better I stay this way,' he added, laughing.

'But even today, when anyone falls seriously ill in their family, they do the Hindu Satyanarayan Pooja,' said

Dhondutai, '…not in their home, of course, but at a neighbour's house,' she added, with a secretive smile.

Later, I discovered that it is a common practice among many Muslim musicians to trace their lineage to the Hindu saint-singer Haridas Swami. There really should be no reason for this revisionism, for Indian classical music has been the site of a wonderful confluence of Hindu and Islamic ideologies and traditions.

In fact, it is almost impossible to accurately trace the genealogy of Indian classical music. There is no written history to go by, only sculpture, paintings, and crumbling manuscripts. A scholar who has spent the last twenty years trying to compile an encyclopedia of Indian music has been confounded by the stunning absence of factual information. Was the sitar invented by the Persian poet Amir Khusro or does it have local Indian roots? What is the origin of the word aalaap, which refers to the slow cadences with which a musician lays out the raga? Some Muslims insist that it comes from 'Allah aap' (Allah, you respected one). And did a particular raga come from Persia or was it always Indian given that the same melodic framework may exist under two names in India and Persia respectively?

The truth is, no one quite knows. Like a tumultuous river, this music has gathered different influences along the way and merged them into its flow. Most musicologists agree that the basic scale came from the sage Bharat Muni, who lived some time between 500 BC and 500 AD. Ancient Vedic chanting used three notes, later five, then seven. The chants developed into organized groups of notes which eventually became ragas. Just as in the west, music emerged as a medium to praise divinity. In India, organized music was initially sung in temples. The compositions praised God; the audience was comprised of devotees. Gradually, between the twelfth and fourteenth centuries, the music moved to the royal courts and developed into a sombre, stately style called dhrupad. The texts of the compositions also started to change. For instance, the music sung in the temples was about the gods, while what was sung before the king was in praise of him.

Indian music was transformed quite dramatically around the thirteenth and fourteenth centuries when a series of Muslim dynasties, culminating with the Mughals, established itself in north India. The cultural landscape began to change. Elements from Islam inspired the architectural aesthetic, dress habits, food—and of course, music—irrevocably altering its rendition. A musician and poet called Amir Khusro, who was of Turkish origin but lived in India, started melding Islamic motifs into the local music. He inspired many new ragas, drawing from Persian melodies. He also created new genres within the dhrupad style, replacing traditional Indian compositions with Persian verses and couplets. Both Hindus and Muslims regard him as a saint-singer.

Although Islam was the dominant faith of the ruling class in north India, people didn't define themselves by religion. Rather, class and caste, both spillovers of a deeply embedded feudal system, were more divisive than faith. Many poor Hindus converted to Islam because it offered them an opportunity for social mobility. Some others converted for reasons of patronage. These converts included a number of professional musicians, such as Alladiya Khan's ancestor.

Music evolved as a remarkably syncretic space. Hindu musicians converted to Islam but performed in temples. Muslim rulers became enthusiastic patrons, but were unmindful that the compositions being sung in their courts may have been in praise of Hindu gods and goddesses. In fact, the Mughal emperor Akbar, commissioned compositions in the local Hindi dialect rather than in Persian. In the mid-nineteenth century, the Nawab of Oudh, Wajid Ali Shah, an epicure, poet and musician, known for his pluralist beliefs, wrote:

'Hum ishq ke bande hai / Mazhab se nahin vasta...'
We are slaves of love, not of religion...

By the end of the nineteenth century, most musicians had converted to Islam, essentially because their patronage came from Muslim kings and nobles—at least in northern India. The legendary singer Tansen, was born Hindu, but once the emperor Akbar adopted him into his court, he converted. Born Ram Tanu Mishra, he became Mia Tansen and the texts of his compositions changed from evocations of Hindu gods to praises of Muslim saints. But like his cosmopolitan patron, Akbar, he had both Hindu and Muslim wives, and children who followed both religions. Above all, his music remained sublime.

So, was this music Hindu or was it Muslim? The question is irrelevant. In the eighteenth century, a singer called Niyamat Khan, who called himself Sadarang, introduced a number of khayal compositions which come closest to Indian classical music as we know it today. The introduction of decorative elements in khayal—which literally means thought and imagination—is considered the single most important Muslim contribution to music by those who prefer to define musical genealogy along religious lines.

What developed, however, from the sixteenth century on was a gradual syncretization of music in north India. Alladiya Khan may have been Muslim but he, or some member of his family, performed every day at the Mahalaxmi temple in Kolhapur as part of his duty to the king and the people. Another well-known Muslim family of dhrupad singers, the Dagars, sang regularly in the inner chambers of a famous temple in Rajasthan which was out of bounds even to high-caste Hindus. Their music, not their faith, was their offering to the gods.

With the growing involvement of the royal patrons, music moved from being a medium of prayer to a form of high art. The performer was no longer the religious singer, but an entertainer. This change also marked a lasting divide between north and south India—creating two distinct styles of Hindustani (northern) and Carnatic (southern) music—which exist even today. While music in north India gradually changed its aesthetic and purpose, classical music in the south, which was fairly removed from Islamic influences, continued to play a religious role and retained many of its original compositions. Even today, Carnatic music resembles the temple music that was sung many centuries ago.

It was only during the early twentieth century that the notions of 'Hindu' music or 'our' music came into the picture. The British, who had mastered the statecraft of divide-and-rule, set the ball rolling. In their obsession to document the history of the 'natives,' British ethnographers started to record India's cultural history. They divided everything into 'Hindu' and 'Muslim', ignoring the more ambiguous confluences that expressed themselves everywhere—in architecture, music, dress, even in a new language. The defining moment came when the British conducted an exhaustive census of the country, and added a new category to their survey—religion.

They thus ordered and revised India's history, and religion became a marker for identification. The new Indian political elite fell into the trap and started to identify themselves as Hindu or Muslim. Suddenly, the idea of being Hindu became paramount and part of a new cultural nationalism. In order to survive in the public domain, performers may have had to renegotiate their identities along religious lines.

In the late eighteenth century, Sir William Jones, published *The Musical Modes of the Hindoos*. He argued that there was nothing to be learned from the 'muddy rivulets of Mussalman thinking' and that Indian music history had been preserved by Hindus; music as a means of cultural expression, reverted to its 'sacred' Vedic origins. Most musicians at the time were Muslim. It is possible that Muslim artistes like Alladiya Khan were forced to find refuge in Hindu identities as a strategic measure to survive in the public domain.

By the turn of the century, two acclaimed scholars of music, Vishnu Digambar Paluskar and Vishnu Narayan Bhatkhande, began to align music with a nationalist agenda. Paluskar was driven by a mission to rescue music from illiterate and debauched musicians 'who performed it for the dissolute entertainment of indolent princely state rulers'—which is how a right wing Marathi newspaper put it.

Their agenda fit snugly into the larger political dramas of the time. The nationalist struggle, followed by a savage partition, forever scarred relations between two communities who had long lived—and sung—together. Without realizing it, numerous Hindus become suspicious towards Muslims—even if they happened to be their beloved teachers. In this case, the best strategy was to adopt them as 'Hindu-ized Muslims' which is what one suspects happened with the Alladiya Khan family.

'Alladiya Khan used to wear the sacred thread of the Brahmins,' Dhondutai often said. 'He was so Hindu, he rarely drank tea, let alone touched other vices.'

Dhondutai, and many other singers, routinely speak of 'Hindustani classical music' as 'our' sacred music and emphasize the Hindu-ness of their Muslim teachers. Even a highly educated sitar player once said to me, in a back-handed acknowledgment of Muslim contribution to this art form: 'This may be our music, but it has been kept alive by them.'

'You are too young to understand these things. Do you have any idea what happened to us because of them?' said Dhondutai in a burst of anger, echoing millions of Hindus for whom the myth of hatred had grown larger than the reality. As a young teenager, I thoroughly enjoyed arguing with the figures of authority in my life, and Dhondutai was a prime target. But when I saw her expression, I remained quiet. 'Our home would have been razed to the ground and my family finished, if it wasn't for divine intervention.'

She then told me the story about how her house in Kolhapur had almost been burned down by a raging mob. She was about twenty-three at the time.

It was 1948. Mahatma Gandhi had just been fatally shot. The assassin, Nathuram Godse, was a right wing extremist who believed that Gandhi had undermined the Hindu population of India.

Kolhapur's ruling elite has a mixture of two Hindu communities—the Marathas, who were descendents of the Kshatriya kings, and the Brahmin priests. For the longest time, the division of labour between them was clearly defined. The kings ruled, and the priests prayed. There was mutual respect and both needed each other. However, somewhere along the way, a wily group of priests, the Peshwas, grew powerful. They started manipulating the kingdom from behind the scenes.

The Maratha warriors were jealous and bitter about the emerging power of the Peshwa Brahmins. The smallest excuse would spark off problems between them—especially in places like Kolhapur, which was predominantly populated by the Marathas. So, when a Brahmin murdered Gandhi, the Marathas went out with their pitchforks and swords.

Dhondutai was at home with her grandmother and sister when her mother came running in, screaming, 'They're burning down the homes of Brahmins down the street! What do we do? They are going to kill us!' The men were out. The women cowered in the kitchen, desperately trying to decide whether they should run out, or risk being burned alive in their home.

'What should we do with all the grain in the store-house?' wailed Ayi. 'The gold for the children's weddings is lying in the trunk upstairs. Go get it!' Besides their own wealth, the family had in their possession, gold and important papers belonging to Ayi's brother which he had left in their safekeeping when he moved to Hyderabad to set up a pharmaceutical business. Along with theirs, another household's treasury would be lost.

In front of the house was a small pagoda which had been set up for wedding ceremonies, for Ganpatrao would rent out his lawn for wedding parties. 'If the pagoda catches fire, it will flare up instantly. It is made of dry straw,' said Dhondutai. 'We'd better get out of here quick.'

The women grabbed whatever they could lay their hands on and came out on to the street. In the distance, they could see smoke rising out of homes on which the crazed mob had flung crude kerosene bombs. People from the neighbouring houses had also run out on the street, but they were not worried. Almost all of them were Maratha. The neighbours crowded around Dhondutai's terrified family and reassured them that nothing would happen to them. They had all been good friends. They had attended each other's birth ceremonies and mourned together when someone died.

Then a miracle happened. A man came sprinting down the road and stopped in front of the house. He came up to Dhondutai. 'Don't worry, tai,' he panted. 'I know these people. I will make sure your house is protected.' Dhondutai looked at him in despair. 'Please, please see what you can do, brother.'

The man was a Maratha buggy driver. For the past ten years, he had been ferrying Dhondutai and her father to and from the railway station whenever they went out of town for a concert. He also happened to be a music lover.

He pushed the family back inside the gate and stood there. By the time the mob approached the street, they had already lost steam. The driver shouted to the goons leading the crowd, 'These are my people. It's alright. Move on.' They did, and the family was saved.

But the riots across Maharashtra succeeded in sending people into their communal cubby holes, secured by fear and hatred. Suddenly, neighbours who had trusted and loved each other, became suspicious and fearful. Some Brahmin families lost everything and had to start their lives from scratch. Men, who had once got by as teachers or small-time priests with patches of farmland, were impoverished overnight and forced to move to bigger cities and find demeaning jobs in offices that had no interest in their past.

Things would never be the same again. People became more conscious of not just religion, but also their caste. Soon after this, even the Kulkarnis decided to pack up and move to Hyderabad, where Ayi's brother offered them all jobs supervising the making of medicine in his successful ayurvedic business. Dhondutai and her sister would be especially valuable to him, as the medicines often required raw materials like rare gems and semi-precious stones and he needed someone trustworthy to ensure that there was no pilferage.

'But baiji, it was your own Hindu Maharashtrians that did this to you, not the Muslims,' I protested, with all my liberal might. 'Then why on earth blame the Muslims?' I was an argumentative sixteen-year-old, and our lessons nowadays were often filled with long debates on modernity, communalism and politics.

'Yes, but it happened because of the Muslims. It was because of them that Gandhi became weak and that is why he was murdered,' she said sharply. 'And it was because of his death that the riots happened. You have no idea what we Hindus went through.'

It was so easy. When things get bad, you create a perceived enemy, especially when there is already resounding endorsement from all quarters. The myth grows greater than the reality. All human beings do it—personally and politically. But I persisted in trying to get her to change her perspective.

'How can you have such vicious views when all your music has come from a Muslim family?'

'They were not really Muslim,' she said, and we were back to the old tired tale of how Alladiya Khan used to wear the sacred thread of Brahmins.

Three

Dhondutai's flat finally came through two years after she put in her application. The house was allotted in Borivli, a fast-growing suburb north of Bombay, in a vast apartment complex called Prem Nagar. Dhondutai happened to answer the phone when an officer from the department of culture called with the news. Her heart leapt when she heard him say that her keys would be handed to her that Friday afternoon. The flat is walking distance from the railway station, he announced. He knew that this seemingly minor detail could make or break a real estate transaction in Bombay.

Dhondutai cancelled her Friday lesson and got ready to leave right after lunch. She put on her watch with the black strap which she only wore when she went out. She put a fresh handkerchief into her purse and zipped it slowly. Manjutai and Dada wished her luck and joked, 'Make sure you come back to your other home in a hurry.'

She laughed and made her way down the teakwood stairs. As she sat on the train, she mentally started to calculate the time it would take for her to get to her new home from Manjutai's house.

She got off at Borivli station, walked slowly up the stairs, crossed the pedestrians' bridge and climbed down again. When she walked out of the station, she looked around her and tried to acclimatize to her new surroundings. She could buy her fruit and vegetables here, she thought. Things are usually cheaper near the station. She started walking westwards, following the instructions given to her, past the bus depot and the roundabout. She asked someone the way to Prem Nagar, just to reconfirm, and finally entered the quiet colony that would soon become her permanent address. She looked at her watch. It had taken her one hour from the time she had left Shivaji Park. The officer was waiting for her in front of block D.

'Kulkarni madam?'

'Yes, that is me.'

'Welcome. This is it. D wing. You are on the third floor.' He pointed up to a tiny balcony that could barely accommodate one person. 'The building is only one year old. Most of the people who live here are jewellers and traders from Gujarat. Come, let me take you upstairs. Watch your foot, there is a step here.' He led her into the elevator which immediately belted out a shrieky jingle bells tune when the door opened—a common feature added so that people would not forget to close the door behind them. The apartment was on the far end of a dark corridor which already bore signs of aging.

It had three rooms and a kitchen. The apartment layout was remarkably unimaginative, for all the rooms lay on one side of a passage. Light and ventilation were subjects that had clearly not crossed the architect's mind. But for those who have experienced homelessness, these things do not matter. When he handed over the keys and asked her to sign a document, Dhondutai was overwhelmed with emotion. She paused with the pen in her hand, shut her eyes, and silently mouthed a quick prayer. After years of moving from one temporary home to another, she had a place she could call her own. The only problem was that Borivli was far away from the life and people she knew, but she would find a way around that.

She didn't move in right away. Instead, she visited the flat once every other week and lovingly dusted its window sills and kitchen counters. Every time she went there, she bought something new to stock her kitchen. It took several months, one utensil at a time, to fully equip the place. Various household items were gifted to her by her students. My mother presented her with a wall clock. Manjutai gave her a tea set. Another student, Manjula, bought floral-patterned fabric to make into curtains. It was only after Dhondutai had bought herself an altar, this time one bigger and more elaborate than the one she had in Kennedy Bridge, and installed it in her kitchen, that she considered spending the night there. A house without the gods to protect it could never be called home. She called her old priest to conduct a small ritual, installed all her gods, and was ready to move in.

She then began to spend every weekend in Borivli. After the Monday morning rush hour had wound down and the stations became gentler spaces, filled with chattering housewives out on shopping excursions, Dhondutai would make her way back to Shivaji Park, where she continued teaching her students through the week.

When I first came to the flat, I felt like I had entered a sparsely furnished play-house, painted in pastel shades. The sky-blue kitchen had two tiny shelves, a small cupboard, and a three-hook rack on the wall. The altar was installed there, in a prominent corner, beside the granite platform.

The pale pink living room was bare, except for the bed and coffee table that had plodded through two homes in the city and finally reached this nondescript suburb.

The next time I went there, I encountered the familiar faces that had guided me through my lessons over the last six years. Through her neighbours, Dhondutai had found a carpenter who did odd jobs in the housing colony. She asked him to hammer three nails into the wall in the hall. On one side, she put up the sepia photograph of her parents. Next to it, the enormous portrait of Kesarbai, her white pearls gleaming. On the other side, she put up a montage of the whiskered, weather-beaten faces of the Khansahibs. There were three generations of Alladiya Khan's family, each member more imposing than the other, with his coiffed moustache and tall turban. This was her lineage. These were the people that had taught and inspired her, and they would always look after her, for death is merely a physical parting. Whenever Dhondutai was low, she would turn to her father in the picture for support, and she would hear his words telling her that the goddess would take care of her. Or, she would look at Bhurji Khan for a blessing and then be able to spin out a taan that had been stuck in her throat. Sometimes, they spoke to her in her sleep. Sometimes, they just smiled at her from the walls. Dhondutai was never alone.

Four

I went to Shivaji Park every Wednesday, and to Borivli every other weekend. My lessons were not very regular, as twelfth grade Shakespeare and first kiss daydreams were taking precedence over ragas and taal. Somehow, however, I never stopped going to Dhondutai. She was like my third grandmother.

While walking towards Manjutai's house for my lesson one afternoon, I noticed that a part of Shivaji Park was being cordoned off. A police van was parked on one side and a couple of officers were standing around, munching peanuts. I crossed the street and walked up to a peanut vendor to find out what was going on.

'Who knows? Some programme,' muttered the vendor, with an air of indifference.

'It is something to do with the Babri mosque,' said a man standing next to him. 'It is a concert for communal harmony. They are going to sing a song called 'Hindu-Muslim bhai-bhai,' he added, guffawing. He back-slapped his friend who was standing next to him and they both laughed raucously.

Bombay had suddenly been divided into ghettoes defined along religious lines. Shivaji Park, headquarters of the Shiv Sena, was clearly marked 'H.'

'I hope you are going to attend,' I retorted, catching the

man by surprise. He was clearly not used to insolent young women. He mumbled something to his friend and they both started to walk away. The friend responded by turning around and licking his lips, puckering them in my direction. I scowled at him and walked away, disgusted with everything that was happening around me—this ugly face of sexual aggression and religious aggression, sometimes not so distantly linked.

The concert had been organized by a group of activists who were disturbed by a series of events that was changing the way India behaved. The right wing BJP had recently decided that the site of a crumbling mosque in Ayodhya was the birthplace of Rama. The party had then mobilized that eternally available army of unemployed twenty-somethings to storm the mosque, and break down its dome with pickaxes. The result was a series of horrific riots across the country, including Bombay, which had always proclaimed itself as cosmopolitan.

The protests against this hideous violence were surprisingly muted and restricted to mostly intellectuals. One group of theatre activists decided to show their protest by inviting musicians, painters and dancers to participate in an all-night vigil and express their support through art. The venue chosen was Shivaji Park, a public garden in the heart of Bombay which, ironically, was named after the warrior king who had been coopted as an icon by the Shiv Sena. The activists organizing the vigil called themselves Artists Against Communalism.

I came back later that evening with my parents. The concert began with the Dagar brothers, a duo that continues to sing the old dhrupad style. Their slow, guttural chants filled the air, as Shivaji, astride his cast iron horse, melted into the twilight. He had to disappear; a family of Muslim musicians was singing what was once a Hindu temple art form and making a mockery of communalism.

It was a full moon night. People had spread rugs on the grass, and sat cross-legged or lay reclining against cushions, listening to the music. The musicians sang on through the night, people from different faiths synchronizing their hearts and notes. Every so often, a flock of white doves fluttered out noisily from the branches of a giant, ghostly banyan tree behind the stage, their sleep disturbed by the music. They fanned out into the sky and circled above the stage before settling back down. Passers-by drifted in and out. Some stayed on, others had to catch the last train home.

As I wandered around the park to stretch my legs, I ran into my friend, West, an American who had adopted India and was learning Indian classical music on the guitar. We went for a walk and picked up glasses of hot tea from a vendor on a bicycle.

We met another acquaintance, Narayan, who was closely connected to the music world. A dance performance which we weren't particularly interested in came on and we walked into an empty parking lot nearby where West started to roll a joint with practiced ease.

'It is so amazing to see how artistes manage to transcend the rifts that divide ordinary mortals,' I said, wide-eyed, all of seventeen, and about to experience my first loaded cigarette.

'That is because this music circulates in another plane, where the spirit is forced to surrender to a higher power. Have you heard the story of Bhaskarbua Bakhle and the great Nathan Khan?' said Narayan, taking a drag.

He was referring to two of the greatest musicians ever, whose music died with them as they lived in the pre-recording era.

Nathan Khan was one of the most popular singers in the early twentieth century and would get invited to sing in princely courts all over the country. Bhaskarbua was desperate to learn from him but could catch him only for brief stints when Nathan Khan was passing through his village in Dharwad. In those days, Bhaskarbua was staying in a house that belonged to his uncle, a crusty Brahmin, who spent most of his days praying and wandering from temple to temple. This uncle was frightfully conservative. If he was walking on the road and even the shadow of a low-caste untouchable crossed his path, he would rush to the nearest river and bathe. He carried with him, at all times, a vessel of water and sprinkled it on the ground wherever he suspected a low-caste person or Muslim had treaded.

One time, Nathan Khan dropped in to visit his protégé Bhaskarbua. He arrived in the evening. They sat down to sing. After some time, Nathan Khan asked for dinner, insisting on the richest mutton dishes. He also needed his wine and sheesh pipe. Bhaskarbua was utterly distressed. He knew that such things were sacrilege in the home of his uncle, but he also had to abide by the wishes of his teacher. Nathan Khan drank and smoked through the night, between singing and teaching. They slept on the floor, amidst a mess of empty decanters and ash droppings.

They had slept only a few hours, when Bhaskarbua woke with a start. He remembered that his uncle would be walking past the house at the crack of dawn, after bathing in the river. Sure enough, when he looked out of the window, he saw the familiar figure in the distance, walking towards the house, clutching his brass vessel and probably muttering prayers. Bhaskarbua panicked. He shook his teacher awake and said, 'Please Khansahib. You must leave, and I will try and clear up this mess or I will never be allowed into this village again.'

'What's the matter, son?' Nathan Khan rubbed his eyes and asked gently.

'My uncle is on his way. He will kill me.'

Nathan Khan yawned and scratched his testicles. 'Bring me my tanpura.'

Bhaskarbua scurried across the room, tripping over his dhoti, picked up the tanpura, and brought it to his teacher. In a few seconds, Nathan Khan started singing an ode to Shiva, set in Raga Bhairavi. Bhaskarbua was transfixed by his teacher's singing and surrendered his fate to the god of music. From the corner of his eye, he saw the door open and the silhouette of his uncle against the emerging dawn. The figure continued to stand there. About fifteen minutes later, Nathan Khan put down the tanpura and looked up. The old priest entered and touched the great singer's feet.

He said, 'I have been praying to Shiva for the past sixty years. Today, I felt like I actually saw him. Thank you, Khansahib.'

We walked back into the concert in silence. There were fewer people in the audience and we settled down close to the front. The musician on stage was singing a haunting Sufi poem about universal love. The song implored people to follow their hearts, and not the politics of the moment.

By five in the morning, the park was almost empty. My parents had left a while back and I had begged them to let me stay on with West and his friends. Only a scattering of die-hard listeners and the organizers remained. About the time the first crows began cackling, and the sky started turning a deep shade of indigo, a famous singer came on stage and started chanting a Sanskrit prayer. He then moved to a beautiful khayal and ended with a short plea to the forces above to bring sense to his people. He was Muslim. Or was he? I don't remember.

Five

I rang the bell to Dhondutai's flat in Prem Nagar, Borivli. A few minutes passed. No answer. Another unbelievably long minute, and I feared the worst. The door wasn't padlocked outside, which means she was definitely inside. What if she had slipped and fallen and was lying on the floor, paralyzed? She was alone in her new apartment. What if some stranger had pushed his way into the flat and done something horrible? A flurry of ghastly images flashed across my mind, when I heard the click of the inner door. It slowly opened, and I saw her small frame against the wire mesh. Her left arm was in a sling. I walked in, shutting the door behind me and said, 'Oh no! baiji! How did this happen?'

'Don't ask! Come on in,' she said, with a laugh.

I touched her feet, as she sat down, wincing slightly. 'I fell two days ago. I slipped on the wet bathroom floor and went for a nice toss. I have a very slight fracture in my left arm.'

Have you been to the doctor?'

'Doctor? Pah! I went, but I can handle this myself. I know more than these doctors do. They just take money and tell you to keep coming back so that they can extract some more. I can manage quite well, except for one thing,' she smiled. 'It is impossible for me to wear my blouse without straining my arm.'

I then noticed that Dhondutai had no blouse on, and her sari was wrapped tightly around her bare shoulders. It was strange to see her pale nakedness. She saw my expression and laughed.

'My part-timer can help me with it, but I just don't bother. I am carrying on with life and work, and music, exactly like before. The more you feel morose and sick, the more the illness says, "Aha. Here's someone who will welcome me into their home, so I will stay longer!" You have to be strong and move on.'

I stared at her in amazement. In front of me, in a fresh blue sari, was a five-foot-something, sixty-year-old soldier. When she sat on the couch, her feet didn't even make it to the ground. But she wore an armour built out of loneliness and fierce independence. She continued her tirade against modern medicine.

'Besides, I am perfectly capable of administering my own medicines. You do know about my medical background, right? I once ran an ayurvedic pharmacy for my uncle in Hyderabad—for seven years, no less! It runs in my blood. And healing is a lot about instinct and experience, not what you cram in colleges. Come on, dear. Enough chit-chatting. Sit down to sing.'

She continued to chatter as I pulled the tanpura out of its sleeve. 'My grandmother was an illiterate woman but she had learned natural medicine on her own, and had a formidable reputation as a healer. She would walk all the way to the outskirts of the village where the low-caste untouchables lived and help them if they were sick—at the risk of making herself unpopular among the Brahmins. On her way back, she would take a dip in the Panchaganga river to purify herself. So, you see, healing is in our blood.

And I firmly believe there is a link between music and medicine.'

'But baiji....'

'Forget all that,' she cut me off. 'The more important thing is what the papers have to say about last week's concert. They are all praises, not just for me but also you. Read it. After this, you will see why I tell you to give up your foolish studies and focus on something you are uniquely gifted with. Anyone can go out and get a BA. This, only you can do. And it is an insult to God to throw away a gifted voice. Come on. Read it aloud.' She beamed with pride.

She had laid out three newspaper clippings on her table, one in English from *The Times of India* and the others in Marathi. I picked up the English one and read the music critic's review of Dhondutai at the Kesarbai memorial concert at the prestigious Dadar-Matunga Cultural Centre. It praised her liberally. As I read it out, she glowed, although she only understood a few scattered phrases, like 'lightening-fast taans' and 'combination raga.' In the last paragraph it concluded: 'Dhondutai was accompanied by her competent students Namita and Manjiri. Manjiri gave her good support on Raga Bageshree. Namita (17 years) who shows great promise, shone in Raga Hindol-Bahaar, and especially in Bhoop. Her resonant baritone voice and complex taans were reminiscent of the great Kesarbai Kerkar, which was apt because the concert was held in her memory.'

'Now let those others go and eat their heart out'—and she named her favorite competitors, with a chuckle. 'Let's see what students they can produce. There are not too many of your age who can do what you do. Give another ten years. If you persist and do what I tell you, you will go places.'

As she went on about the concert, my thoughts went back to that exhilarating evening. I had worn a white Bengali sari with a red border and slipped on my contact lenses instead of my thick glasses. As my mother and I were leaving the house, my father turned to us and said, 'Our daughter has grown into a fine young woman, what do you say?' I felt grown up.

We walked into Dadar-Matunga Cultural Centre. I caught the familiar aroma of jasmine and hair oil. A number of people were already there, sitting patiently on the carpets laid out in front of the stage. Manjutai's husband Dada sat on the side. He waved to me as I walked in, tripping slightly over my sari pleats. 'Be careful,' he called out, smiling.

When I greeted Dhondutai, she smiled and said, 'You're looking nice! Make sure you go to the bathroom before we start.' She gave me her purse to hold while she went to take care of business. When she got back, she sent me on the same mission.

I clutched the tanpura gingerly while we filed onto the stage behind her. Dhondutai made me sit on her right, Manjutai on the left. Extremely self-conscious from the time the organisers announced my name and someone handed me a small, cellophane-wrapped bouquet of wilting roses, I fixed my gaze on a few members of the audience without really focusing on them.

On the far right of the stage, there was a gigantic portrait of Kesarbai—the same image as the one that hung on Dhondutai's wall. A garland of fresh white flowers hung around it, chosen by Dhondutai, who knew her teacher's preferences better than anyone else.

I sang just a few short pieces when she gave me the

signal with a short movement of her hand. She had me sing more on the lower octave because it showcased the timbre of my bass voice. Later, when it was time for the taans, I knew I did well, because she turned around twice and said, 'Wah! Good job, beta!'

Dhondutai's sari slipped off her shoulder for a second and I saw her bare vulnerable arm. I put the newspaper clipping back on the table and began to strum the tanpura. I sang the opening notes of Hindol-Bahaar, the same raga that had won me my first critical acclaim. I didn't have the heart to tell my teacher at the time, that I had just been admitted to Princeton University's undergraduate program, and would be leaving the country in less than five months.

Part III
The Khansahibs

One

It was six in the evening when I got to Dhondutai's flat in Borivli, one evening in early December. The crows were cawing tunelessly outside her window and the familiar sweet and spicy smell of Gujarati cooking drifted out of the neighbouring balconies. She was hanging her clothes to dry on a nylon rope strung across the length of her flat. I had flown in from New York a day earlier, and was meeting her after a gap of almost two years.

Whenever I went back to Dhondutai, I felt I was entering a space that was timeless. Nothing changed. The same black-and-white television set layered with dust; the plastic milk bottle with a spray of fake flowers that I had gotten her years ago; the pictures on the wall of Kesarbai, her parents, Ganesha and the Khansahibs; and her other everlasting companions, the tanpuras. In deference to modern life, she had acquired a refrigerator at some point, but even that remained mostly bare.

It was utterly reassuring—like going back to your childhood room many years later, and finding your teddy bear perched exactly where you left it, with its left eye still hanging loose. For me, Dhondutai was like that stuffed toy, unconditionally affectionate and always around. I went back to her and was at peace. We would tune the tanpura and pick up where we had left off.

She looked the same. Her hair was still black. The only difference was that she had a small gap in her teeth, the only hint of her vulnerability to age. I didn't hesitate to do something that I had earlier been uncomfortable doing—I touched her feet. I suddenly valued her more than I did the Nobel laureates who showered me with their brilliance in Princeton's Gothic ivy-covered lecture halls. Here, I was sitting at the feet of the master.

I began to strum the tanpura, delighted to run my fingers against the familiar strings and melt into the swirl of notes. At university, I practiced whenever time permitted and performed occasionally at the campus's International Center. My tanpura, which stood in a corner in my dorm room, elicited rude remarks—'phallic symbol' and 'voodoo object'—from some of my white American friends. I ignored the jibes and played against being exoticized.

Dhondutai asked me how my parents were, and about my sisters. Neither of us was really interested in the pleasantries and quickly moved on. She said she would teach me Raga Multani, since it was that time of day—this particular combination of notes resonates with the shadows that emerge when late afternoon merges into early evening. It was a raga I was not familiar with. She explained that it was from the Todi family.

'Notice how the notes of Multani are almost the same as that of Todi, which you have already learned,' she said.

'Then what is the difference between them?'

'Aha! That is the beauty of our music,' she smiled. 'Just imagine, dear. There are only seven notes and thousands of ragas. The differences between two ragas are sometimes so subtle—merely an extra emphasis on a note, or the interval between two notes—and yet, the two ragas will evoke entirely different moods and stories. Now, the main difference between Todi and Multani is the use of a single note, pa. And Todi is sung mostly on the lower octave, which is why it is a morning raga, while Multani revolves around the higher notes, so it is sung around this time in the evening.'

'All this,' she continued, 'is in our heads. We never wrote anything down.'

'Wow,' I sighed, with the awe of one who could only relate to memory in terms of gigabytes.

'We had to remember everything, the similarities, the differences, the areas to watch out for where one raga could easily slip into the other. The secret is that when you are singing a particular raga, you have to train your mind to pretend it is the only raga you know.'

I told her about a famous sitar player I had met a few months ago when he had come to play at Princeton. He had been experimenting with a performance technique in which he was trying to separate the conscious and subconscious mind, so that the conscious mind could innovate while the subconscious mind effortlessly played out the notes. For this, he suggested that the musician practice while watching television or engaging in some other mindless activity. While his mind would superficially engage with the soap opera or whatever was on, his playing would become almost automatic. This would help him master the techniques so that, when it was time to perform, his conscious mind could freely focus on the creative process and direct the subconscious mind to follow instructions.

Dhondutai nodded and smiled. 'Well, I don't quite agree with that. Our music is too difficult and complex for such experimentation. You have to focus all your energies on it, or you will go terribly wrong.'

She loved the fact that I had an opinion on everything. It challenged her. It made her feel like she was working with someone who was not a parrot, like many of her students, but truly appreciated the reasons behind everything—as long as it lay in the realm of music. Yet, she preferred to have the last word.

The Multani composition she had begun to teach me was beautiful: Hai re man, kaahe ko soch kare re? (Oh restless mind, why do you think so much?) Soch kare kachhu ban nahin ave, dheeraj kyon na dhare re? (By thinking or worrying, nothing will change. Instead, have faith... and patience.)

The words resonated with the tumultuous experiences I was going through as I entered adulthood—first love and first loss, moving away from the sphere of one's parents, and the gradual process of self-discovery that comes when you leave home and learn new rules, unlearn old ones. I was trying to put into practice what had been written thousands of years ago: try your best and accept the rest. I had learned how to have faith and not be ashamed to say so.

I was moved by this intimacy between great music and Indian philosophy. There was so much about tradition that didn't have to change for the sake of changing.

'This composition is special. It was the first piece Bhurji Khan taught me.' Bhurji Khan, the son of Alladiya Khan, was her first teacher. I was excited to be introduced to the very music that had been my teacher's initiation raga.

'Baiji! Tell me more! How old were you when you started learning from this family? What was he like as a teacher? Did you fidget as much as I used to? What made you pick him and this gharana?'

She laughed and said, 'Listen, then... I started learning with him when I was thirteen years old.' She stopped for a moment, as if pausing and rewinding a memory spool. 'But before him, I had done a short stint with Alladiya Khan's nephew, Nathan Khan. And then, of course, there was Baba...'

And so, I heard the story of the maestro Alladiya Khan and his family through the eyes of Dhondutai. I heard the tale of how he founded the Jaipur Gharana. I listened, fascinated by how a young Brahmin girl was taken into the folds of a musical Muslim family like an adopted daughter, and allowed to inherit its secrets and treasures. Dhondutai told me, with an ironic smile, that she had to be born outside this family to receive the treasures of their music. If she had been a blood daughter, she would have been given nothing. Because she was a girl.

Alladiya Khan was born in 1855. His real name was Ghulam Ahmed, but he came to be known as Alladiya, which literally means 'given by Allah'. His parents had lost several children before him and had gone to a holy man to make sure that this child lived. He did, and they believed he came with God's grace. By the turn of the century, he had become a living legend.

Alladiya Khan lived during a period of political upheaval. The British were comfortably embedded in India, the jewel in their crown. Under the colonial government existed an intricate network of princely states ruled by maharajas and nawabs who were more or less compliant with their foreign rulers. As long as they passed on a prescribed share of their revenues to the British, they were given some token independence. These princes were encouraged to pursue a life of royal decadence—which included hosting a regular stream of court performers.

Thus, the princely states became the main source of employment for musicians and other entertainers; mimicry artists, painters, dancers and wrestlers. Some princes genuinely cared about the arts, but most were driven by vanity and a competitive urge to showcase the best performers in their courts. Exaggerated stories about their flamboyant generosity were whispered all over the country and became part of common lore. Did you know so-and-so king was once so pleased with a flute player, that he paid him his full weight in rupees, along with an elephant? And one maharaja was so moved by a performance that he spontaneously paid the musicians the entire amount that had been reserved for his army, just before going to war!

The time of princely patronage has been romanticized as a glorious period for Indian music, but musicians didn't always have a good time. Most spent their days travelling from court to court, before they found a ruler who really appreciated their art. Sometimes, even if they were employed in a particular court, they had to travel to supplement their income. If a king died, and his successor wasn't as interested in music, or favoured cock fights as a form of entertainment, the musician would be out of a job. Patronage was often arbitrary and erratic. Very often, the prince favored women performers who could also double as mistresses—for them or their ministers.

Besides, patronage came with its own idiosyncrasies and depended on the individual ruler's temperament. For instance, a famous king, Sayajirao Gaekwad of Baroda, compiled a book of rules called *Kalavant Khatyache Niyam* (literally, 'rules for the artiste's warehouse') for court performers. The artistes were slotted in categories which determined their salaries, what they could wear, when they could go on leave, and what they were to perform. Sayajirao, who was quite taken by British ways, also introduced the idea of notation in Indian music, a concept unheard of until then. In fact, Alladiya Khan had visited the Baroda court, and would have stuck around as a court singer, but when the minister in charge of performing arts brandished the idea of notation in front of him, he ran away.

Like many other musicians of that period, Alladiya Khan and his younger brother Hyder Khan were regulars on the circuit, moving from one kingdom to another, wherever they got a 'gig.' They would travel on horseback or on camel, depending on the terrain. Hyder Khan had to learn how to wield a sword, just in case they got attacked by robbers or wild animals on their journeys—which happened once, in the deserts of Rajasthan. They were on their way home after a performance, when a troop of bandits stopped them and demanded their money. Khansahib quietly told his brother that they should cooperate and they handed over their purse. Before leaving, the bandits happened to ask the brothers where they had gotten the money. When they found out that they were musicians, they asked them to sing. At first the duo was nervous, but as they warmed up, they forgot where they were, or who their audience was, and sang a sublime raga. The bandits were so moved by the music, that they returned not just the Khansahibs' purse but also gave them whatever other stolen jewels and money they were carrying!

The centre of patronage was in and around the courts of Delhi, but other notable kingdoms on the musical map were Gwalior, Baroda, Jaipur, Patiala, Mysore and Kolhapur. In the early nineteen hundreds, Kolhapur was ruled by a young king called Chhatrapati Shahu Maharaj. He was barely twenty when he inherited the throne and he died in his forties. But in his short life, he achieved great things—he encouraged education and lower caste assertion, and he supported the arts. It was a time of great well-being in Kolhapur for, as they say, if the king loves music, there will be peace in the land. Kolhapur was dubbed 'Kalapur,' city of the arts. Shahu Maharaj had an uncanny ability to spot artistic talent. Painters, musicians, even wrestlers, thrived in the state.

Shahu Maharaj's younger brother had as a lover a courtesan called Krishnabai Kolhapurkarin. She had decided that she wanted her daughter Tanibai to learn music from the great Alladiya Khan who, by then, had established himself as a powerful singer. But the Khansahib lived in faraway Bombay. The young prince was very keen to please his favorite mistress. How could he get the great Alladiya Khan to come to Kolhapur? The only way was by asking his brother, the maharaja, to hire Alladiya Khan as the court singer of the state.

Once, he and his brother happened to be in Bombay together, and he heard that Alladiya Khan was performing somewhere. He grabbed the opportunity and took the maharaja to the concert. Not surprisingly, Shahu Maharaj fell in love with the Khansahib's music. He felt he would be an asset to his state and invited him to be his court musician.

So Alladiya Khan and his family moved to Kolhapur around 1895. The king gave him a house and agreed to look after his brother and other family members. Alladiya Khan's official duties included singing at a temple in the old palace and performing for the maharaja. Any private engagements could be accepted only with the king's permission. His brother, Hyder Khan was also appointed state singer and his nephew, Nathan Khan was given the job of singing every morning at the ancient temple by the river.

Over the next twenty-five years, Kolhapur's stature on the musical map of India grew tremendously because of Alladiya Khan. Musicians moved there just to be around him. One such singer, Rajabali Khan, moved into a house right next to Alladiya Khan's home so that he could secretly listen to the Khansahib while he practiced and then try and copy his style. He did this for years, until his singing actually began to sound like Alladiya Khan's music, and he even became a well-regarded performer. Finally, Alladiya Khan persuaded the king to send the plagiarist away. Shahu Maharaj requested the king of Dewas to take Rajabali Khan on as a court singer, and everyone was happy.

The maharaja grew very fond of Alladiya Khan and his family and wanted them around him all the time. The Khansahib's three sons, Nasiruddin, Badruddin and Shamsuddin, who were better known as Badeji, Manji and Bhurji (literally, meaning the big one, the middle one and the one with curly hair!) spent most of their time in the royal palaces. They played with the young princes and ate with them even though they were commoners. They were treated not as subjects but as the princes' companions and were dearly loved by the king. The king even ordered his children's tutor to teach the three boys Sanskrit scriptures, especially the ones that were relevant to music. The Brahmin teacher would say, 'Yes, sire' to his face, but he could not bring himself to commit such a monumental act of blasphemy—teaching Muslim infidels sacred Hindu texts—and he would find some excuse or the other not to tutor them.

One day, after listening to a particularly moving concert by Alladiya Khan in the palace courtyard, the prime minister pulled the king aside and said, 'Sire, I have something important to discuss with you. It is all very well that you are bringing up these young boys as if they were your own. But do you think this way they will be able to learn any music from their father? Who do you think will carry on this tradition if these boys turn into decadent prince-like creatures?'

The king was stunned into silence. He was unwittingly finishing off a musical legacy. If these little boys weren't trained from the time they were young, the music would die with their father, for great singers like Alladiya Khan passed on their best musical secrets only to their own blood. This musical lineage had to be preserved.

'But how can I possibly ask them to leave? I don't think I can bring myself to say it,' the king said, looking troubled.

'There is only one way,' the prime minister suggested. 'You know how proud these boys are. You will have to insult them so that they themselves leave in a fit of anger.'

'Hmm. A good idea. See! This is why I need a minister like you to advise me,' the maharaja smiled.

A few days later, a small-time prince from a neighbouring kingdom came to visit Kolhapur. That evening, Shahu Maharaj sent a message to the Khansahib's three boys that they could not eat with the royal guest. This had never been said to them before. They were outraged, particularly the young Manji Khan, who was known for his temper.

134

They went up to the king and Manji huffed, 'We don't need to eat with you. With our music, we can buy fifty-six kings like you.' They stormed off and never returned.

The king's courtiers were horrified at the boys' insolent outburst. No one spoke to the maharaja like that. But Shahu Maharaj merely smiled. He had achieved exactly what he wanted. And, sure enough, each of the boys went on to become great singers.

'... especially Manji Khan and Bhurji Khan,' said Dhondutai, as she finished her story. She got up and walked over to the portrait of Alladiya Khan and his family that was mounted on her wall, next to the ones of her parents and Kesarbai. She took the tail end of her sari, stood on her toes, and dusted the glass frame. 'Poor Badeji never quite made it. I can't begin to tell you what happened to him. It is the worst tragedy...' she said, pointing to a serene, older face in the picture.

'What happened, baiji?' I asked, intrigued.

Badeji was turning out to be an accomplished musician for, as the eldest, he had received the best training from his father. One hot afternoon, Badeji was playing cricket and the ball hit him right on the chest. He vomited a little blood. Worried about his growing prowess as a singer, some rival musicians went to a local doctor and bribed him to give an incorrect diagnosis about Badeji so that he would never sing again. The doctor told Alladiya Khan that his firstborn had a weak heart and would not be able to survive a life of singing. From then on, he was not allowed to exercise his vocal chords and was sent, instead, to Uniyara, the family's hometown near Jaipur, to look after their land and property.

Dhondutai snorted and narrowed her eyes. 'What a joke. He had a perfectly healthy heart and lived to be almost ninety.'

Manji Khan, the middle one, was the maverick. He became a great singer and was the only one in his time who wore suits and roamed around Bombay in his own car. Unfortunately, he didn't live beyond fifty. When he died, Alladiya Khan was still alive and was devastated. He said, 'God, today you have taken away not just my son but with him, an irreplaceable treasury of music. The goddess has just put one foot outside the gharana.' His utterance was prescient. After him, the lineage slowly faded out.

This was more interesting than the Indian history class I was taking in Princeton. I looked outside and felt that the tulsi plant in Dhondutai's balcony had begun to resemble the periwinkle that I had grown to love in the garden outside my dorm room.

She said, 'According to me, there are three people in this family who really contributed towards keeping this gharana alive, by teaching as many people outside the family as they possibly could—Hyder Khan, Bhurji Khan, and Baba.'

Dhondutai's eyes were brimming over. I began to strum the tanpura softly, realizing that it was time for me to rescue her from the dead weight of memory.

Two

I first met Baba many years ago, when I was a little girl and Dhondutai still lived in the flat under Kennedy Bridge. He was a soft-spoken man with thick eyeglasses, who wore loose white pajamas that flapped around his ankles.

He was sitting on her couch in his cotton undershirt and pajamas, slurping hot tea from a saucer, when I walked in. Every few minutes, he took off his glasses and wiped off a film of mist. I noticed a blue, weather-beaten attaché lying under her coffee table.

'Touch his feet,' Dhondutai whispered to me.

I was always wary of being coerced into the rituals of obeisance that came so naturally to members of the music world, but reluctantly obeyed, scowling at the floor as I did. Baba patted my shoulder warmly and gave me a wide grin that made his opaque glasses twinkle and transformed him instantly from foe to friend. Dhondutai stood beaming on the side, her hands interlocked on her arms, as she often stood. 'Now wait till you hear her sing. She is my little Kesarbai...' she said.

I sang Raga Bhoop for Baba, and happily noticed that he responded to my full-throated rendering with great enthusiasm. After I finished a fifteen-minute presentation, I put the tanpura down, and gleefully waited for the two of them to lavish praise.

'She really is very promising,' he said, and looked at me. 'I hope you are going to take your gift seriously.'

'Of course she is. At least someone will take this gharana forward, unlike all those fools you have been teaching, who have made a hash of your grandfather's music.'

Baba was Alladiya Khan's grandson. He had grown up amidst a musical galaxy of father, uncles, and, of course, grandfather, but unlike them, he had never become a performer. Every time he sang with some intensity, his blood pressure went up. So he took to whistling instead, and could render the most complex ragas and melodies!

He still lived in Kolhapur, in the ancestral house which had once been awarded to his grandfather by the king. But he had not been able to keep the family legacy alive. The bungalow, which had once resonated with ethereal music, was falling apart, crowded with numerous family members and discordant voices. There was no place for music in a world where princely patronage was long gone, and people had to work in factories and offices to earn their living. The tanpuras and tablas had been wrapped in old cloth and stored away in a backroom. Every once in a while, a singer of the Jaipur Gharana would come to Baba to learn one of the rare ragas he had inherited from his grandfather, and Baba would generously share his knowledge.

Whenever he wanted to replenish his soul, or just get away, he would catch a train to Bombay and come to Dhondutai. It was on those visits that I met him, year after year. Every time we met, his expectations of me remained as enthusiastic as ever. And all three of us continued to indulge in the delusion that I would be a great performing artiste one day.

'So how are you enjoying America?' he asked, twinkling, when we met again years later.

'Great fun. I am meeting all kinds of brilliant people. But I miss my music,' I lied, to please him and my teacher.

'Yes, yes. Nothing can match this. I hope you keep practicing while you are there,' he said, looking at me through his thick glasses and smiling widely.

'I do, whenever I can,' I said, but when I sang that evening, it was fairly obvious that I rarely did.

Baba was about Dhondutai's age, maybe a few years older. There was a tender familiarity between them, that which comes when two individuals have known one another in an age of innocence, before each enters separate worlds that beget squawking children, professional dis-appointments, monthly budgets, and life itself. I had always wondered about the possibility of a sexual tension between them. Had there ever been any undercurrents that crossed the boundaries of friendship? His children called Dhondutai Atya, which is the name given to one's father's sister, and the relationship was thus defined by this nomenclature, but couldn't there have been one moment of weakness? Perhaps one night, when Ayi was sleeping, and they stumbled into each other in the dark passage in Congress House? I wanted to let my imagination run its course, but I knew that when it came to Dhondutai, it was a futile exercise. She walked the narrow path. There were no grey areas.

Baba lay down and started to read the newspaper while Dhondutai disappeared into the kitchen to make dinner. A few minutes later, she returned with the rolling pin in her hand and a frown on her face.

'Baba, tell me, are you still dropping in on that donkey, Kunti? Even after all the games she has been playing and the lies she tells about who she has learned from? You know very well what I am talking about.'

'Yes, Dhondutai,' he replied, smiling sheepishly, for he knew he was treading on dangerous ground. 'I will be visiting her place tomorrow. She wants me to teach her a few things. How can I refuse? She is from our gharana.'

'At least treat this music with some respect. It is not to be distributed to the undeserving. You know, Baba, sometimes I feel you are really foolish. Everyone simply takes advantage of your good nature,' Dhondutai admonished him, oblivious to my presence, or to the fact that he was the son of her first teacher and automatically occupied a position of respect in the hierarchy of her music world.

He didn't reply because he knew she was right. His thick eyeglasses hid large brown eyes filled with the kind of disillusionment that settles into one's being like a benign tumor.

Even though they went through long spells of not speaking to each other over some petty squabble or the other, they had been there for each other at crucial moments over the years. When Dhondutai moved to Bombay with her mother, it was Baba who called an old doctor friend and asked him to introduce her to his spiritual guru, Swami Satyananda, an enlightened soul who lived in a remote ashram outside the city. He knew that she would need some sort of protection from the ill-wishers and musicians who envied her lineage. They would be sure to try and jeopardize her chances of getting into the performing circuit and spread malicious rumors about her. So, the Swami took her under her wing and gave her the guidance and support that takes one through difficult times.

Above all, it was Baba who introduced Dhondutai to Kesarbai, that fateful day when her life would change for ever.

As for her, she had helped Baba out whenever she could, slipping envelopes crammed with notes into his hand when she saw that he needed it. She had even tried to give back the gift of music to his family, first by teaching his son, and later his grandson, who came to learn with her briefly in Bombay.

She took liberties with Baba as one would with an old friend. Yet, on another level, Dhondutai revered him as her guru. Not only was he her teacher's son but, over the years, Baba had passed on to her a number of rare ragas and precious compositions. Long after his father and grandfather had died, he continued to share with her these gems, when she came to Kolhapur or when he visited Bombay.

When she still lived in Kolhopur, Dhondutai would spend long hours with Baba each day. Anyone walking into the Kulkarni household between five and seven in the evening, would be enchanted by what he saw; three musicians sitting across from each other on the hardened mud floor, singing, chatting, learning and laughing. They were Dhondutai and Baba, both in their twenties, and a much older man called Ganpatrao Gurav, who accompanied them on the tabla.

Late one evening, Baba was teaching Dhondutai Paravati, a rare morning raga. The raga is very close to a more popular raga called Lalit, and the notes appear to be the same, until the surprise twist which introduces a pa.

'Baba, what are you doing? That is not the right way. You are so funny!' said Dhondutai giggling.

'Oops, you are right. I made a mistake,' said Baba, fingering his toothbrush moustache nervously. 'I'd better refer back to my book.' Baba screwed up his eyes as he peered into his little book of compositions.

The camaraderie between Baba and Dhondutai went well beyond the fact that they were man and woman. There was love, yes. But it was a love triangle, really, between man, woman and music. Sometimes, when Baba's wife stood behind the door, watching the lesson, keeping her two young sons from running into the room, she felt a wincing pain within her which she couldn't place. It was the knowledge that she would never be able to share with her husband the closeness that Dhondutai had, because she couldn't speak their language.

'Aha. I think I have found what I was looking for,' said Baba.

'How can you be my guru!' said Dhondutai, rolling her eyes in mock disapproval.

While the two youngsters were joking around, Gurav stopped playing and said, softly, 'Both of you are wrong. Let me tell you how it goes.' He shut his eyes, as if to jog his memory, and sang the composition correctly, though a little off key.

'Yes, yes, that is right,' exclaimed Baba. 'That is exactly how it goes.'

Gurav smiled, thrilled that he had been able to contribute his two bit and the three resumed the session. It is hard to place a precise value on Gurav's knowledge of music, for it was the kind that seeps in unsolicited, sometimes even unbeknownst to its recipient. Gurav had played the tabla with Alladiya Khan. Over the years, like many accompanists, he had imbibed the nuances that even students do not have access to. It was the kind of knowledge that a spouse or child picks up through sheer proximity to the head of the family, from overhearing conversations, or watching him at work. Baba, who had never been a concert singer himself, could only teach the pieces in their abstract form. The combination of Baba and Gurav, however, was immensely valuable to Dhondutai and she gradually built on her repository of rare ragas.

Teaching sessions often went on until dinner time, and both Gurav and Baba would be invited to join the family for dinner and would relish Ayi's cooking over endless discussions on music. Sometimes, they would pull out a long-playing record of some great singer like Zohrabai or Ustad Abdul Karim Khan, wind up the gramophone, and sit around listening to the sounds of genius.

By genetic default, Baba carried within him a tradition that was both massive and magnificent. He was certain that if he didn't pass it on to the right musician, it would be lost with him. His descendants had already foregone their musical legacy and merged into a nameless, faceless multitude. The family tree was withering, and the gharana was coming to an end.

The gharana is one of the most touted features of the Indian musical tradition, though some argue over its contemporary relevance. Literally speaking, gharana comes from the word ghar, or house, and extends into clan or family lineage. But in the musical context, it has a far more complex meaning. It is a stylistic construct. Also, it is the quick marker with which musicians identify and place one another.

There is nothing quite comparable to it in the western world, but some scholars have compared gharanas with the various intellectual schools of thought in Europe. The difference is that the gharana is based on a single personality. It tends to grow around a creative master whose genius and originality attract musicians, connoisseurs and aspirants into his fold. Those who adopt the master's style follow his musical principles with unquestioning exactitude. If the particular style survives a couple of generations, it is recognized as a new gharana.

A gharana is thus a lineage of hereditary musicians and the particular musical style they represent. It is generally named after the founder's hometown or the place where he flourished. For instance, the Agra Gharana, is named after a city which was famous not just for the Taj Mahal, but for the great court musician, Faiyaz Khan, who was born there in 1880, though he spent most of his life in Baroda. The oldest gharana, the Gwalior Gharana, was founded in Gwalior, a city which has a history of music-loving kings. And the Jaipur Gharana came to be because its founder Alladiya Khan originally sang in the Jaipur court.

A gharana was also the logical product of princely patronage. Since the rulers wanted the best performers to grace their courts, a musician's individuality and repertoire became his asset, with a value attached to it which could command a price and salary. It became important for musicians to create distinctive styles which would distinguish them from others, so that they could secure better positions. These specialized styles and compositions would then be zealously guarded, like copyrighted software, for it was through them that the artiste and his descendants insured their livelihoods.

Every gharana has a personality which reflects the temperament, aptitudes and eccentricities of the founding master. For example, the Jaipur Gharana developed its peculiar style quite by default. It emerged as a result of a handicap that afflicted Alladiya Khan. One day, while Baba was visiting Dhondutai and tales of yore were being exchanged, he told me the story.

In his early days, long before Alladiya Khan came to Kolhapur, he served as a court musician in the princely state of Amleta. He had been there only six months, but the king was besotted with his music and commanded him to sing for him night and day. The Khansahib finally lost his voice. He was so depressed over his condition that he considered suicide; music was his life.

At that time, one of his well-wishers suggested, 'Killing yourself is the easy option. Why don't you, instead, convert this into an opportunity to create something special and unique despite the condition of your voice.'

That was when Alladiya Khan conceived of a style of singing where even if the singer's voice is not exceptional, the music is so spectacularly complex that it will hold the audience's attention.

The Jaipur Gharana is thus universally regarded for its intellectual weight. It prides itself on a rich repertoire of rare and complex ragas and, especially, compound ragas which seamlessly meld two or more ragas, highlighting the features of each one, to create an entirely new sound.

The gharana is not just a stylistic orientation, but also a repository of ragas and compositions, regarded almost as immovable property and must be kept in safe custody the same way a wealthy matron would safeguard her jewels. Just as a direct heir has the right to inherit family wealth, so this intangible wealth was kept only for the blood relatives of the founder—that too, usually for the male. In fact, many compositions have never even made it to public concerts because they were reserved for select patrons or taught secretly to special disciples who were almost always close relatives. Sons came first, then nephews and cousins and sons-in-law.

Marriages were carefully and strategically arranged to ensure that the music remained within known territory. For, even the daughter of the house was exposed to this wealth from the time she was born and, by default, she too carried the family jewels. She was never officially trained but picked up the knowledge by being a fly on the wall—or a wife in the next room.

The women's knowledge of music was not to be taken lightly. Dhondutai told me a story about one of the senior Khansahibs (Alladiya Khan probably, or Jehangir Khan). When the old man used to sit down to teach his sons, he never announced the raga he was teaching them. He would just start with a slow rendition of notes, and then stop to take a drag from his sheesh pipe, after which the boys had to identify the raga and pick up where he'd left off. If they got it wrong, they were in trouble. Just after their father started, they would fight each other to run into the kitchen on the pretext of refilling his sheesh pipe so that they could grab their mother and get her to identify what was being sung. And she was never wrong.

A musician's child's paternity was established not by how he resembled his father, but by how closely his music did—as a story famously describes. The son of one Amir Khan once ran into his father's friend at a music conference. The friend, Balakrishnabuwa, a veteran singer himself, was resting with his eyes closed, when the young singer went up and introduced himself as Amir Khan's son. Without opening his eyes, he said, 'Show me.'

The surprised youngster said, 'Well, if you open your eyes, you will see how much I resemble him.'

'Let me see how much your music resembles his.'

So the young man started singing. After a few minutes, the old man got up, opened his eyes, and said, 'I can see you are Amir Khan's son. In fact, even your features are remarkably like your father's!'

By and by, people with no musical background or family connection to it began to want to learn music seriously as well. Bhimsen Joshi ran away from home to learn from the legendary Sawai Gandharva and became an embodiment of the Kirana Gharana. Alladiya Khan taught Mogubai and Kesarbai. Hariprasad Chaurasia was born into a family of professional wrestlers who could hardly be affiliated with something as effete as a bamboo flute!

The notion of gharana thus gradually moved from being simply familial. After all, Dhondutai was not remotely related to Baba by blood. She would not even touch a glass of water in his home, because meat was cooked in his kitchen. But they both harboured and protected the family property with the same pride.

Three

It was late in the night. The fireflies had gone to bed. The village kulkarni or rent collector was up, writing his accounts. As he sat in his office room and wrote in the light of the flickering candle, he found himself nodding off to sleep. He rubbed his eyes, got up and walked out of the room onto the porch. He heard the sound of anklets tinkling and a shadow crossed the outside wall of the house. Peering into the darkness, he saw a woman walking. It was Shakuntalabai, a well-known singer of lavani, going home after a performance. He beckoned her to come and sing for him so that he could stay awake. She laughed and agreed, and he then got back to work.

A few minutes later, he looked at the paper and was horrified. He had been so moved by her plaintive voice that, instead of writing the names of the farmers and the amount of land they owned, he had been writing words from her song on the state's embossed stamp paper. How could he possibly go to the rent minister with his ridiculous story and ask them for new stamp paper. He was certain he would lose his job.

The next day, the rent collector went around collecting the rent in a frenzy. He managed to collect a thousand rupees but, as usual, some people hadn't paid and asked for extensions. So, he put in his own money to make up for the missing amount, and proceeded to the revenue minister in the city of Kolhapur. The officials were pleased to get the full rent because it was so rare for the amount to come in all at once. Seeing that he was in a good position, the rent collector decided to take a chance and disclosed what had happened to his stamp paper. The officials laughed and replaced it immediately.

The rent collector happened to be Dhondutai's grandfather, a man whose passion for music was inherited by his only son, Ganpatrao, Dhondutai's father. Although the family profession involved land revenue and accounts, which earned them their last name, Kulkarni, they all harboured a love for music.

Ganpatrao was a schoolmaster. In between his official duties, he wandered around learning music from a number of teachers. His chosen instrument was the tabla. He decided that, even if he couldn't become a serious performer, his firstborn—whether boy or girl—would learn how to sing from the best guru there was.

Dhondutai was born in 1926, at a time when it was unheard of for a Brahmin girl to be connected with the performing arts. Women who sang in public were usually from the courtesan community who, although respected on stage, were clouded by an unspoken truth. They were bais, who essentially earned their living by pleasing wealthy men. Girls from 'good' families were not to go anywhere near them. In spite of disapproving murmurs from his community, however, Ganpatrao decided that his firstborn would sing.

Besides loving music, he was driven by a secret belief which he never voiced in public. Classical music had fallen into the 'wrong' hands—those of the Muslims and the courtesans. But it had sacred Vedic origins. His view was unequivocal: Hindus had to get their music back.

By this time, the Alladiya Khan family had established itself as the pride of Kolhapur. Aspiring singers had already moved there from various parts of the country to learn from the Khansahib, his brother, or his nephew.

On Dhondutai's fifth birthday, Ganpatrao said, 'Dhondaram, today we are going to meet a very special old man. Tell your mother to get you ready. We will leave right after my prayers are over.'

Ganpatrao used to call his daughters by boys' names. Dhondutai became Dhondaram and Shakuntala, her younger sister, was Sakharam. They may have been lovable nicknames, but underlying them was a powerful sentiment—one which perhaps set the tone for Dhondutai's future. Ganpatrao believed in equality between boys and girls. Whether it came to their education, or upbringing, or marriage, he did not differentiate between his daughters and his son, Babu.

That morning was the first time Dhondutai encountered the Khansahibs.

When they got to Alladiya Manzil, a young boy wearing khaki shorts and a vest was playing marbles outside. 'Baba, where is your chachu? Take us to him,' said Ganpatrao. Baba ran inside. Ganpatrao and his little daughter followed him.

Inside, a woman pulled her head scarf over her face and disappeared into an inner room. The father-daughter duo sat on a low bed. Baba's curiosity got the better of him and he stayed inside, standing against the door shyly, placing one foot on top of the other. Soon, Nathan Khan, Alladiya

Khan's adopted nephew, came out and greeted them. When he heard why Ganpatrao had come, he shook his head. The venerable musician did not relish the idea of teaching one so young. 'Sorry,' he told them. 'She is too small to absorb anything.'

Ganpatrao was resolute that his daughter's training begin, so he did something unusual to indulge his passion—he persuaded a friend of his, one Bakhre, to go and learn music from Nathan Khan and even paid for his tuitions. He was afraid that once Nathan Khan left, there would be no one good enough to teach his daughter. His plan was that at least Bakhre could learn some of the specialties of the gharana, and later teach them to his daughter.

But Bakhre and Nathan Khan's lessons did not quite take off. Eventually, Nathan Khan found out why Bakhre was coming to him; he was a proxy for the little girl he had turned away. He laughed and said, 'Come on, I'll teach her for fifteen minutes every day. That's as much as she will be able to learn at this age.'

One evening at dinner, a few months after Nathan's Khan's lessons began, Ganpatrao noticed that Ayi was not her usual self. She was slapping the rotis onto the banana leaf plate rather than placing them lovingly the way he had been used to since she had first entered his life as a terrified twelve-years-old bride. She rarely lost her temper and the two of them had established an equation of love and understanding that was rare for the times. He was sixteen years older than her and almost a father figure. Then why this silent tantrum? Could it be that he had been out in the rain and not paid attention to his health? Could it be that he had scolded his son Babu for getting up late? He stared at his pretty young wife questioningly but she averted her eyes.

It was only later in the evening, when he sat on the porch outside his house, listening to the crickets and humming a tune in Raga Bhairavi, that Ayi came and stood next to him, without saying a word. He was lost in his world, and until she sneezed did not even notice her presence.

'Aaho…'

'Listen…'

They both spoke simultaneously. Then, they lapsed into silence for a few seconds. Finally, Ayi spoke up.

'I met Ansuyatai this afternoon. She had dropped in to give me some brinjal from her garden. She was telling me about a girl who had acted in a school play, won an award, and had her picture published in the local paper, and what a commotion it had caused in her family because they thought her marriage prospects were doomed.'

'Aha! So that is what all this is about. Dhonda's music lessons.'

'Everyone is talking about how you are sending a young girl to learn music—that too from a Mohammedan. Which decent Brahmin boy would marry a girl who has been spoiled like this? There is a limit to your eccentric ways. Remember, your daughters are daughters, not sons. Please stop this Dhondaram and Sakharam thing.'

Ayi started sobbing. Ganpatrao wanted to say something, but didn't. He got up and walked into the house. His heart reached out to his wife, but music was a mission beyond all emotions and social obligations. If need be, his daughter would not get married. His wife should know better than to argue. She knew he was not like the rest. After all, he had even taught her how to read and write, at a time when women did not learn much beyond the secret of creating a hearty masala rice.

Dhondutai's lessons with Nathan Khan continued as before. Although the Khansahib sat with Dhondutai for only fifteen minutes every day, his tutelage was so thorough that within a couple of years she was winning local music competitions, and became the pride of the Padma Raje girls' school. She was allowed to miss her classes if she had a concert and even started singing on the radio, earning her first few rupees at the age of eight. People took notice of the child artiste, and a film producer approached Ganpatrao to get little Dhondutai to act in his next film. But the good Brahmin knew where to draw the line. He knew that he would really be inviting trouble if he allowed his daughter to become a screen star.

Nathan Khan left Kolhapur when Dhondutai was eight years old. He was pulled away to Bombay by a then upcoming actress called Durga Khote, who wished to learn music.

Dhondutai's childhood was spent running around the garden, chasing butterflies with her little brother and sister, or helping her mother in the kitchen. In the evenings, after dinner, the children gathered around their grandmother, Aji, who told them stories about gods and goddesses while the flickering light of an oil lamp threw out shadows on the walls and made the stories come alive.

There were strange links between gods and humans. Their lives were often intertwined, so that the gods sometimes behaved like base mortals and the humans sometimes became divine. Like the children's favorite story—about Dattatreya, the three-headed child god, who lived in a tiny temple where five rivers meet, a few miles outside Kolhapur.

'Many years ago, when there were only jungles everywhere, and birds were often messengers from the heavens, there lived a pious sage called Atreya Muni,' their grandmother whispered.

'He was our ancestor. We are from the Atreya gotra,' interjected Ayi, while rocking Babu, the youngest, on her lap.

'Your mother is right,' said Aji. 'Now, Atreya's wife was called Anusuya, and she became known for her unconditional devotion to her husband. The bored goddesses in heaven were tired of constantly hearing about her goodness and her piety, and they decided to test her. So they sent their husbands, Shiva, Brahma and Vishnu to earth, disguised as wandering monks, and told them what to do. They wanted to see whether she would be goody-goody even under dire circumstances. The gods arrived at her hut, disguised as Brahmins, and asked her for food. But they demanded that she be naked when she served them. Anusuya was in a fix. How could she turn down the holy Brahmins? On the other hand, how could she comply with their demand? Her husband was out meditating by the river, and wouldn't be back until much later. But her wits saved her. She sprinkled water on the three men, chanted a mantra, and turned them all into toddlers—just like little Babu here! Then, without any hesitation, she undressed and served them a delicious hot meal!'

The children blinked sleepily at their grandmother, wonderstruck by the tale.

When the goddesses figured out what had happened to their husbands, they were horrified. They sent a messenger to bring the gods back. Meanwhile, Atreya Muni, who was thrilled to see the three greatest gods of the universe playing in his house, built a temple dedicated to them.

'And that's how Dattatreya, the three-headed child god, came to be worshipped at Narasimhawadi, where the five rivers meet. Your father will take you there to show you the temple,' said their grandmother, yawning. 'That's all for now, children. Time for bed.' But all three children were already fast asleep, dreaming of white elephants leaping across the skies, carrying child gods.

The following Thursday, Ganpatrao sent a message to Nathan Khan that he should not come to teach that day. He was taking his family to visit Dattatreya. He had been meaning to go for a while. Little Babu had a bad stammer and he wanted to appeal to the child god to help him overcome it. The last time they had been there was to give thanks when Dhondutai was born.

Ayi packed a hearty lunch in banana leaves. The family was going by bus—except for Ganpatrao, who decided to swim across. On the bus, Ayi and the children munched on freshly roasted puffed rice, seasoned with salt and mustard seeds and a sprinkle of grated coconut. A group of pilgrims sitting in front broke into a beautiful song praising Dattatreya, playing castanets to keep the beat. Ayi, who rarely let herself go, chimed in, prompting Dhondutai and Shakuntala to cover their mouths and burst into giggles.

Like most things in life, it is unclear which came first— the holy confluence of the five rivers, or the Dattatreya shrine. The site of the temple was magical and serene, the silence broken only by temple chimes, guttural chants and the musical splash of someone diving into the river below.

The shrine was at the end of a large parapet, twenty-one stone steps up from the river embankment. It nestled under the long protective tentacles of a gigantic banyan tree. Ensconced inside was a statue of the three-headed god who had been tricked into regression by a clever woman.

When they got there, Ganpatrao had already emerged from the river. He was talking to Tanibai, a singer, who had come from Kolhapur by boat. The family washed their feet and hands in the river, and went up to pray. Ganpatrao made them sit in front of the shrine. He himself stood, hands folded, and started singing an abhanga, a robust hymn, while his children clapped in time. Tanibai came up to them and said, 'Wah! What a musical family. Is this the little girl learning from Khansahib?'

Dhondutai smiled shyly at her. Something about this spot made her feel exhilarated and the same feeling would come back to her every time she returned.

When the sun was high up in the sky, they all slept under a tree, lulled by the water lapping against the steps below. They got up in time for the evening prayers. Ganpatrao prayed for his son's health. Ayi prayed that her daughters would find good husbands. As they got up to leave, a breeze wafted up from the river and a bunch of dead leaves swirled into the sky.

Four

Kolhapur had a monumental temple dedicated to Laxmi. Her statue was made of gemstones and was guarded by a fearsome stone lion. Thousands of pillars loomed around her. Some said the ancient structure was built around the ninth century. Others said it was built overnight, by the two door sentries who still stand frozen in stone, when her husband Venkatesh left her for another goddess and moved south. But he continued to visit her there and every night, before leaving the temple, the priest would place a glass of saffron-flavored milk and some betel leaves near the altar for him. By morning, they would be gone.

The temple stood near the banks of the Panchaganga river, behind the old palace of Shahu Maharaj. When Dhondutai was very little, she would climb onto her father's back while he swam across the river near the temple. Unlike any other girl her age, she had learned how to swim and could hold her own in the water by the time she was five.

The king required that someone from the court musician's family perform at the temple every morning before the eight o'clock prayers. It was a special offering, for the gods loved music. Earlier Nathan Khan had been assigned the job of performing at the Mahalaxmi temple. After he left for Bombay, Alladiya Khan's youngest son,

Bhurji Khan was deputed to sing before the altar. Every morning for half an hour, he charmed the goddess with ragas and raginis, and sang of birds and the rain and how Krishna showered Radha with the colors of love.

Devotees would gather there to hear him and to be a part of the prayer session that followed. Among them was a man in a coat and dhoti, with a fair-skinned, rosy-cheeked girl in a red and white polka-dotted skirt and blouse, who sat next to him cross-legged, chin in her hands, intently watching the musician who sang in front of her.

The temple was where Dhondutai began to fall in love with her muse, although she was too young to know it. This goddess would be her shakti, the force that stayed with her for the rest of her life.

One morning, after the community prayers, Ganpatrao approached Bhurji Khan with a request. 'Won't you please teach my daughter? She has already learned under Nathan Khan.'

The Khansahib looked at Dhondutai and said, 'I would need to be paid fifty rupees per month.' Ganpatrao was shattered. There was no way he could afford his fees. He left without a word.

Over the next couple of years, although her vocal training had stopped, Dhondutai learned how to play the harmonium, which is often played to accompany and echo the vocalist. Also, her brother had begun to learn the tabla. That way, her father ensured that their ears would remain tuned to music. He continued to harbour hopes of getting one of the Khansahibs to teach his daughter.

His dream came true quite unexpectedly. On a warm afternoon in 1940, an unexpected visitor showed up at the

Kulkarni household. Ganpatrao was out and Ayi was sleeping. The three children—Dhondutai, Shakuntala and Babu—were playing in the front room. They started when the guest walked in. The little boy nudged his elder sister. 'Look. It's the man who sings in the Mahalaxmi temple,' he whispered.

The children asked him to sit on the special gaddi and automatically touched his feet out of respect. Not knowing what to do next, they stood against the opposite wall looking this way and that, wiggling their toes and staring at the esteemed guest.

'What do you call your father?' Bhurji Khan gently asked Dhondutai, who was now a pretty thirteen-year-old.

'Anna,' she whispered.

'Where is Anna?' he asked, with a smile.

The children had no idea, so they looked at each other and mumbled. Babu dug his nose nervously.

Just then, Ganpatrao walked in. He saw Bhurji Khan and started, as if he had just seen a god sitting in his living room. He ran up to him, knelt before him and said, 'Khansahib! You here? I hope my family took care of you and offered you something to drink.'

Bhurji Khan told him not to worry and simply said, 'From this day on, I will teach your daughter.'

Ganpatrao could not believe his ears. He looked radiant and his eyes brimmed over with tears. But then his face fell, for he remembered the fees required of him.

As if he had read his mind, Bhurji Khan reached out and touched Ganpatrao's shoulder. He said, 'Please pay me whatever you can manage.'

Dhondutai's father paid Bhurji Khan ten rupees every month. By then, the Khansahib had several students who had started earning from their music and could afford to pay him well. One of them was a skinny young man, Mallikarjun Mansur, who went on to become a great singer.

'One more thing...' Bhurji Khan laid down his condition. 'You must not get your daughter engaged or married for at least the next five years. I don't want to later hear you say, "These Muslims took money from us, but didn't teach anything." So think about it and then we will begin.'

Ganpatrao folded his hands and said, 'Khansahib, you have my word. Please start teaching her from today itself.'

Bhurji Khan had decided from that very first day he was approached that he would make Dhondutai his student. But at the time, he had felt she was too young. Instead of saying 'no' outright, he had deflected the situation by asking for a fee that he knew was unaffordable. In those days, people had a strange way of communicating. They often spoke in riddles. Things were not to be taken at face value and life was filled with hidden meanings and cryptic messages. Above all, one had to be patient.

Dhondutai described her first lessons with Bhurji Khan to me and I saw the recurring patterns of scholarship and tutelage that had kept this music alive. She was roughly the same age I had been when I had begun to learn. We both had an obsessive parent who supervised our training and kept us glued to our lesson, even though we would have rather been playing outside. And, for both of us, our first guru was a generous soul who laid strong foundations. After that, the monument had to weather its own fate and destiny.

Teaching is as important a part of the process as performing, for this is what takes this music into posterity.

The books cannot tell you which raga to start with and how to keep time, why a particular taan is not sounding quite right. These are secrets only a guru can give you, selectively, gradually, and when the student is ready to receive them—like the secret of the two-note taan which was whispered to me in the same way that it was passed on to my teacher.

During the very first lesson, Khansahib told Dhondutai that she would have to sell her harmonium. She was wedded to this instrument and knew the black and beige keys as intimately as she did the fingers which had been punching them lovingly for the past three years. Her teacher explained why she would have to give it up.

'Human nature is such that it always seeks easy options. The harmonium makes singing easy because you don't have to work on making independent connections with the notes. By playing it when you sing, you will never learn how to hit the right note with exactitude because you will have this backup—but the reasoning did not fly well with the young girl. Little Dhondu cried for a week after the instrument was put into its case and taken away.

Next, he taught her how to play the tanpura. Her fingers were still too small to command the instrument, but she gradually learned how to strum, and how to hold the tips of her fingers in line with the strings so that she didn't pull at them but glided over them, in a motion that alternated between gently depressing and releasing, depressing and releasing, until it became second nature. He taught her how, when singing, she must always have a composed, pleasant countenance and not gesticulate too much with her hands, which some musicians habitually did. Besides, it was rude to let your hands and fingers fly around in front of your guru. One had to exhibit composure.

Finally, he taught her the basics of the aakaar, the full-throated sound that was the specialty of this gharana. There were two cardinal mistakes a singer could make—one was to go nasal, the other to go out of pitch.

Bhurji Khan had a remarkably creative mind. He would find music in the uncanniest places. There was a beggar woman who came to the gate regularly, with the same cry, 'Mai, Anna-daata ...' She repeated the same two phrases every single day, in the same manner each time, like a broken record. One evening, when he heard her plaintive wail, he stopped his teaching momentarily and said, 'Listen to her. She has perfect pitch,' he added with a laugh. 'I suppose practice makes perfect!'

One day, when trying to explain the importance of hitting the note so perfectly, he said, 'Beta, across the sugarcane fields, there is an ashram. You know it. Your father regularly contributes food and clothes to the students. Go there and listen to them. There, you will find the perfect re.'

On her way back from school the next day, she walked across the field and stood behind the ashram to listen. She was familiar with the place. Her father and she used to go there sometimes to distribute food to the poor boys. The ashram was similar to what a gurukul would have looked like a thousand years ago. Here, she found the students practicing their chants. These were young Brahmin boys training to become priests.

They sang the chants using the notes that were familiar to her, but they sang them backwards on the scale. That is when she heard the perfect re that her teacher had described. She sighed and remembered his words. 'You will find music everywhere if you open your ears and listen. It is the universal language that every one understands. And it is the only language devoid of sarcasm or hatred.'

Bhurji Khan came to her in the evenings, after she was back from school. He began teaching her Raga Multani which was appropriate for that hour. When they graduated from the notes to the verse compositions, the Khansahib was faced with a problem. Young Dhondutai did not know Hindi and most khayal compositions are in the Braj dialect, which is close to Hindi. Bhurji Khan would first simply make her say the words, 'Hai re man…' She had to repeat it forty, fifty times until she got the pronunciation right. He would then explain the meaning to her. It was gradually, through music, that Dhondutai started learning the Hindi language.

Sometimes Baba would come in and sit next to his father for a few minutes to listen to the tutoring, but he was not allowed to speak to Dhondutai. 'Why! He would not even look me in the eye,' Dhondutai said to me, with a laugh. 'If he came across to give his father a message, or to bring something to him, he would enter with his eyes lowered, speak to his father, and leave in a hurry. In fact, I didn't speak to him until years later, when we had all grown up. You see, it was bad enough that he was a young man. What made it worse was that he was also Muslim.' She paused for a long time and I waited patiently.

'It was when Bhurji Khan felt I was ready to start learning the secrets of the gharana that he taught me the two-note taan,' said Dhondutai with a mysterious smile. 'This is the little voice exercise which turns the chakra in your throat and prepares you for the lightning-like taans that are the gharana specialty... of course you know it. I have taught it to you.'

I looked at her quizzically. 'When? You never taught me any secret two-note taan?'

'Of course I have,' Dhondutai said, still smiling. 'I taught it to you when we were still in Congress House and you were very small. You learned how to sing it but you were not aware of its worth. But that is why you are able to sing taans the way you can now.'

I was foxed. I thought back and tried to sing a two-note taan. How on earth can one construct a taan around two notes? I tried various permutations and combinations and found myself floundering. Dhondutai chuckled and wandered off into the kitchen to make tea. 'Keep trying,' she shouted from there. 'Come on. Use your imagination. What good is it going to study in America if you can't figure this out, eh?'

She came back into the music room. 'No luck, still?'

I had pulled and tugged at notes to try and sing a two-note taan, but came up with ridiculous sounds which didn't resemble anything I had ever learned. I begged her to stop the suspense and reveal the secret. She said, 'I will tell you what the two-note taan is, but only on one condition.'

I looked at her and nodded earnestly.

'You have to take a vow that you will never reveal this to anyone except to a student. We have spent all our money— forget money, all our life—learning these things. This is not some Satyanarayan prasad to be distributed free to any person. Besides, you must never give wealth to a fool or someone who doesn't deserve it.'

I made a solemn promise, pinching my throat lightly with my fingers.

She sang it for me and I realized that I had been singing it all my life without realizing it. Whether or not it was really as valuable as she made out was not the point. I made a pledge with myself that I would never betray her trust.

Five

Dhondutai cherished her days with the Khansahibs, especially the few years she spent with bade Khansahib; the big one, Alladiya Khan. 'He treated me like a grand-daughter and he really loved me,' she told me one afternoon, when it was too hot to sing and we had lapsed into chatter.

Among the last memories she had of Alladiya Khan was when he took her to the Vikramaditya Conference in Bombay in 1944, shortly before he died.

The Hindu calendar, called Vikram Samvat, is computed from the time the great King Vikramaditya, won over the kingdom of Ujjain in central India—around 57 BC. This marked the beginning of what some history books have called, India's golden era.

The Vikramaditya Conference commemorated 2000 years since the king's victory. It was part of a nationalist cultural renaissance which had gripped India just before she won her independence from the British. The idea was to showcase the greatest musicians of the country, which then included Pakistan. They came from all over in trains—from Lahore, Calcutta, Madras and Kashmir, with their troupes and their tablas, their shawls and their spittoons.

It was the musical event of the century. There had been nothing like that before and there hasn't been anything as grand since. For seven days, the air reverberated with music. Afternoon concerts merged into evening sessions, and late night ragas heralded the dawn, while the sun's first rays would start filtering in through the glass windows along the hall. People reportedly fell sick from sleep deprivation in their eagerness to grab as many performances as they could. The week-long festival took place at the monumental Cowasji Jehangir hall—which has since been resurrected as a modern art gallery.

A vast private home next to Bombay's opera house—a fifteen minute carriage-ride away from the venue—was converted into a day-and-night mess where food was cooked in gigantic vessels and served all through the day and night for the artistes and their ensembles. Some preferred eating before they performed, some after the show. There was no sense of time as they drifted from performance to rehearsal to performance. A humungous cauldron of steaming tea was perpetually on the fire.

It was at this festival that unknown musicians became overnight stars. A young man from Punjab with a gourd-like stomach and black twirling moustache stole the show with his brilliant renditions of khayal and thumri, and Ghulam Ali Khan became Bade Ghulam Ali Khan, though some suggest that the preface of Bade or 'big' may have had more to do with his physical size rather than his musical stature. A young sitar player from Calcutta, Vilayat Khan, shot to fame and went on to become one of the all-time great musicians of the century. A startlingly unassuming tabla player took the audiences by surprise with his virtuosity. He was Ahmadjan Thirakwa. But it was the vocalists who were applauded the most.

The conference was like a snapshot of all that had

happened in the music world in the last fifty years. Great artistes performed and then, the following day, put aside their egos and accompanied their gurus on stage. Backstage, the harmony was countered by personality clashes and ego battles. The best known fight was the one that took place between Faiyaz Khan and Omkarnath Thakur, both famous singers, who argued over who would sing last, for the chronology of performances was a reflection of seniority and stature. The best always sang last. The decision of who went before whom had led to legendary quarrels which sometimes lingered on for generations, and was carried on by the artistes' students. One musician had left his position as court singer out of fear that the whimsical ruler would make him sing before a lesser musician. In this particular case, Omkarnath finally won—and established his position as arguably one of the finest singers of his generation.

An intriguing couple sat in the front row through most of the performances: an old man with white whiskers, and a pretty girl in her late teens. She wore a traditional nine-yard sari and a blouse with short puffed sleeves. Every one knew who he was—the great Alladiya Khan, but they could not place the girl who sat next to him, attentively listening to the music, her hands neatly folded on her lap. When anyone asked him who she was, he would laugh and say, 'My granddaughter!' But they knew she couldn't be. She wore a bindi—the mark of a Hindu. Some would then whisper among themselves, 'She must be Manji Khan's daughter. He's so modern, he is the only one who will let his girl come out in public.' And if Dhondutai and the big Khansahib heard this, they would just smile at each other.

Dhondutai later told me how Alladiya Khan was able to sneak her into the best seats in the house, which were a thousand rupees each, a princely sum in those days. These front rows of red velvet-lined sofas were reserved for wealthy connoisseurs and maharajas. Many of them bought the tickets because it was the thing to do, but didn't show up. Alladiya Khan could get Dhondutai to sit next to him because there were inevitably empty seats all around.

'Because of his age, he couldn't sit for long stretches. He would make me sit there, go away, and then come back, and I would report every thing that went on,' she said. She dutifully sat there, concert after concert. She described who sang and what ragas they sang. There was one musician who was so restless as a stage artiste, that he started his performance on one end of the stage and by the end of it, had shifted to the other end, she recalled with a laugh.

'There was a singer, Karamat Khan, who was supposedly one hundred and twenty-two years old. I asked the big Khansahib whether he was really more than a hundred years old, and he said, "Yes beta. I don't know his precise age, but I do know he's much older than me."'

'There were very few people Alladiya Khan wanted to spend time with, so he would chat with me a lot. Of course, it was always only about music. He would tell me of the days he tried to become a teacher of Pharsi (Persian) to earn a living right after his father, a reputed singer, died. That was before he joined the family 'business.' After that, he started training seriously under his uncle who would tell him, there should be no relationship between an artiste and a clock and taught him from midnight onward. Until you can translate what your mind wants into your voice, you shouldn't get up from your practice...'

Dhondutai's voice trembled slightly as she remembered her days as a pretty young thing who had the blessings of the greats. I couldn't help the thoughts that passed through me. She had it all—the training, the exposure, the life-long commitment. What had gone wrong? Why hadn't they recognized her as the real heiress of this music? It didn't make sense, and these questions troubled me for years.

The last to perform at the Vikramaditya Conference, in deference to his stature, was Alladiya Khan. 'When he started singing, his voice was slightly shaky, and I remember my heart sinking slightly out of concern that he would falter,' said Dhondutai. He was over ninety years old. Would he be able to sustain an entire concert? A few seconds later, without blinking, he shot off a taan like a lightening bolt. You could almost sense the wave of electricity go through the audience.

That was the last time Alladiya Khan sang in public. Accompanying the Khansahib on the tanpuras behind him, were two people who would become her most important conduits into the music world. The first, Bhurji Khan, had already been teaching her for several years. On the other side was a handsome woman who wore her hair in a side parting and sang like a man—booming, confident.

It was six in the morning and Khansahib had just finished singing Raga Ramkali. After a brief pause, when only the sound of the tanpuras floated into the still dawn, he started the notes of Bibhas, another early morning raga. He then turned around and said to the woman behind him, 'Kesar, this one is for you… Come on, sing.'

Dhondutai got up in the middle of her story and said, 'Wait a second. I'll just be back.' She walked out of the room into her bedroom and I heard the distinctive sound of steel grunt as she turned the cupboard handle. She returned a few minutes later with a withered red and gold brocade pouch tied up with a braided gold string.

'I must tell you another story,' she said. 'While the Vikramaditya Conference was in session, the music organizers had a parallel concert series take place at the nearby Rohini Hall, where younger and lesser known artistes were invited to perform. I also sang there. By then I had become a regular on the performance circuit and was quite well-known…'

That night, she wore her usual white chanderi sari, which she reserved for concerts. Dhondutai sat on stage and looked at her father for approval. She sang Raga Bihag, a night raga, bursting with freshness, exuding all the energy and vigor of the gharana. At the end of her performance, while her father hovered around her protectively, Dhon-dutai shyly met a few audience members. A man in a dapper suit came up to her and said, 'Beta, you were tremendous. I have nothing to give you right now to show my appreciation.' Then he looked at his finger and said, 'Wait. Take this.' He pulled off a ring with a pearl on it and gave it to her. She looked at her father, who cleared his throat and accepted the ring on her behalf.

'Promise me you will never stop singing, my dear,' said the man. Ganpatrao stared after him as he walked out of the auditorium. His friend whispered, 'That is Seth Gopaldas, a close friend of Kesarbai's, and a great patron of music.'

When Seth Gopaldas gave Dhondutai the pearl ring and made her promise to sing for ever, he had no idea that he was unwittingly threading a connection between past and future. Many years earlier, Seth Gopaldas, had been instrumental in bringing together Kesarbai Kerkar and Alladiya Khan. The gharana stayed alive, and he was the one who made it happen. This time he was making another connection. It was one of those moments whose significance only becomes clear many years later.

Six

A year later, Dhondutai, Shakuntala, and their parents were on the overnight train from Kolhapur to Bombay. They were going to spend a couple of months with Ayi's sister, who lived in Mazgaon, an old neighbourhood in central Bombay, in a house squeezed between a Catholic church and a blue mosque.

The day after they arrived, Ganpatrao and Dhondutai went to visit the Khansahibs. A couple of years before the death of Shahu Maharaj in 1922, Alladiya Khansahib had moved from Kolhapur to Bombay and rented a small flat in Surveyor building near Chowpatty, from where you could smell the sea. His son Bhurji Khan who divided his time between Bombay and Kolhapur, where he taught Dhondutai, had also come to spend time with him.

Surveyor was a squat building spray-painted with crimson betel spit. It was populated by a cacophonous medley of khansahibs who came in all shapes and ages. There were old-time singers and even older sarangi players, senior musicians and aspiring singers. Children darted in and out of the entrance, and every time a mother ran outside to grab a straying toddler, she would pull her head scarf below her nose to veil her face. In this community, the women did not expose themselves, and the men were not tempted—or at least that is what everyone pretended.

Ganpatrao and Dhondutai negotiated their way through Surveyor building holding their noses against the pungent smell of meat curry which wafted out of the hallways. The door of the Khansahibs' flat was slightly ajar. They pushed it open slowly and peeped in. Dhondutai was aghast at what she saw. The faint odor of rancid sweat filled the room. Baba stood staring out of the window. On one side of the room lay Alladiya Khan, fast asleep, breathing heavily. His turban and stick lay on a table next to the bed. Next to it, was his sheesh pipe. On the other side, lay a vestige of her teacher, Bhurji Khan. She hadn't seen him in several months. She was aware that he had been unwell, but she had no idea it was this bad. His kurta was soiled. His face was dark and swollen. He could barely speak to her. He smiled at her feebly, and said, 'How is your music, my daughter? Have you been working on that taan in Basanti-Kedar? Remember, it must sound like fireworks exploding into the sky on Diwali night!'

She nodded and managed to smile back. After spending a few moments with him, Dhondutai went into the kitchen with Baba and whispered, 'When did this happen? Why did you not write and tell me he was so ill?'

'Tai, I have been completely out of sorts. It was all so sudden. He has been diagnosed with severe anemia and his kidneys are on the verge of collapsing. The doctor has given him no more than two weeks... I don't know what we are going to do.' Baba pulled off his glasses and dabbed his eyes with his handkerchief.

Dhondutai and Ganpatrao spent the whole morning sitting there, trying to make sense of how serious the situation was. When the senior Khansahib woke up, murmuring Baba's name, Dhondutai jumped to her feet in deference.

'Sit, sit, child,' he said. Those were the only words he could muster. A few minutes later, he shut his eyes and drifted back to weary sleep.

Dhondutai and her father went back to Mazgaon heavy-hearted. Ayi and her sister were waiting for them for lunch. As they sat down to eat, Ayi said, 'What is the matter with the two of you? You look like you've just come back from a funeral.'

'Ayi, you cannot imagine what has happened. Bhurji Khan is on his deathbed. He may not even last to see Guru Purnima. They have tried every thing possible, but the doctors have given up. Even the specialist doesn't know what to do.'

'Oh God! When did this happen? He seemed perfectly fine when he left Kolhapur.'

'It's been a couple of months. Baba has been trying to handle things, but things are pretty bad now.'

They ate in silence. After a few minutes, Dhondutai picked up her plate and walked into the kitchen. 'I am not very hungry,' she said.

Ayi watched her daughter silently wash the dishes. She had her back to her mother but Ayi knew from the slight shudders in her body that she was crying. She went and touched her lightly on the shoulder.

'Dhonda, do you want Shankar Mama to look at Khansahib? You know he is an expert at medical diagnosis. I am sure he will be able to figure out what is going on inside the poor man.'

Dhondutai nodded and dabbed her eyes with the tip of her sari. She went into the other room and picked up her tanpura. She strummed it, and started the base note, but found that when she attempted the next note, she faltered.

She continued repeating sa, trying to derive solace from its magnificent solidity.

Ayi stood at the door, watching. 'I'll talk to Shankar Mama as soon as he gets home this evening. I'm sure everything will be alright.'

Shankar Mama was Shankarao Divekar, Ayi's brother from Hyderabad, who happened to be in Bombay at the time to meet a potential buyer for a new diabetes pill he had developed. Shankarrao was gifted with extraordinary diagnostic powers. He could merely look at a person walking by and tell, by his gait and posture, exactly what his ailment was. He was known to take on cases that all other doctors had given up, just as a challenge, and would tell his patients upfront that if he succeeded in curing them, he would extract a hefty fee. If he wasn't able to, he would take nothing.

That evening, when Dhondutai returned from her walk, she found the family elders sitting in conference, on the settee in the front room. Her uncle looked at her tenderly and said, 'Dhonda, you don't want to lose your teacher, right? Take me to him, dear girl.'

Early next morning, Dhondutai, Ganpatrao and Shankarrao took a tram to Babulnath. Baba was standing outside the door, looking distressed. 'Abbaji's health has taken a turn for the worse. Please come in.'

Inside, under a slow-moving fan, lay Bhurji Khan, motionless, his eyes shut. His father lay on the bed on the other side of the room like an ancient sage, fingering his rosary beads. His eyes were shut and he had a look of serene acceptance. It seemed as if he was singing a silent dirge to his son. He had already lost one son. At the age of ninety-something, he was resigned to accept whatever his god had in store for him.

Shankarrao went up to Bhurji Khan, sat next to him on the bed, and gently lifted his hand. It fell limply into the doctor's custody. He shut his eyes and checked the patient's pulse. A faint frown began to crease his forehead as he fingered the abdomen area, especially around his liver. He put his stopwatch back into his coat pocket and addressed Baba. 'You and Khansahib need to come with me to Hyderabad for treatment. I will give you both a room in my own home. The only condition is that Khansahib will have to do exactly what I tell him. Cigarettes and tea are out of the question. Are you agreeable?' His voice grew softer. 'And of course you don't have to worry about my fees or any thing like that.'

Fees apart, the Khansahib could not even muster up his train fare to Hyderabad. But destiny has its way. Barely ten years earlier, Dhondutai's family had gone to Bhurji Khan, and paid him far less than what his musical tutelage was worth. Today, they would come to the rescue of the dying musician.

Shankarrao gave Bhurji Khan a dose of medicines to give him the strength to travel, and they left for Hyderabad right away. It was a curious little group that sat in the train: four interesting looking men clad in coats and topis, and a young girl in a pale yellow sari, who hummed to herself most of the way.

A long sky-blue Dodge came to receive them at Hyderabad's Kachiguda Station. Ganpatrao greeted Qadri, the old driver. Shankarrao got into the front seat smugly, proud to be driving his guests around in a new car. He and his brother were doing well for themselves, as their herbal remedies and potions were seeing brisk sales and the market was growing.

As they drove through the byzantine alleys of the Nizam's city, Bhurji Khan seemed to perk up slightly. He started reminiscing about a concert in the palace grounds, where he had accompanied his father many years ago. The prince had been so pleased with Alladiya Khan's soulful rendition of Darbari Kannada, that he had spontaneously taken off his ruby necklace and presented it to him, with a heartfelt exclamation of 'Subhanallah!' Bhurji Khan asked if Roshan Ali, All India Radio's local station director, was still around. He had been a good friend to the family and vigorously supported their music.

When they got to the house, Bhurji Khan slowly alighted from the car and looked around him. He suddenly fell to the ground on his knees, his hands raised upwards in supplication. As he knelt on the red mud under the fierce Deccan sun in the middle of Shankarrao's compound, a tear rolled down his eye. Ganpatrao touched him gently on the shoulder and said, 'Come Khansahib. Every thing is going to be alright.'

They helped the weak singer up the stairs in a section adjoining the main house. He and Baba were given a spacious, well-lit room in this wing. There were two cots in the room. Baba took off his father's coat and hat, helped the weak old man lie down, and covered him with a sheet. He then took of his shirt and hung it on a hook on the wall.

Shankarrao came up a few minutes later and said, 'Khansahib, today you may eat whatever you wish, to your heart's content. In fact, I will order your food from the hotel down the road, since you know we don't cook meat and eggs in the house. But from tomorrow, you will be on a strict diet of cow's milk and my medicines for two weeks straight.'

The Khansahib laughed feebly and then broke into a hollow cough. Gasping for breath, he said, 'Oh don't you go about ordering food from outside. A little vegetarian food will do us all no harm! Besides, I am looking forward to bhabhi's cooking.'

'Very well then… Please rest now. You have had a tiring journey. You need to conserve all your energy. Baba, come, let me show you around the house. Treat this place as your own.'

Later that evening, Dhondutai carried a plate of food and a tumbler of water up to her teacher. She stood next to him while he ate, ensuring that he had everything he needed. After he had washed up, he requested her to sit next to him and render a night raga.

'Baba, go get the tanpura. Let me hear my daughter sing.'

Dhondutai sang Basanti-Kedar with the gusto that is reserved for those one loves dearly. The composition was about springtime and new life, and it seemed to touch the cells in her ailing teacher's being, coaxing them to revive and multiply.

For the next two weeks, she visited him every day, in the morning and evening, and sang at his feet to keep him entertained. He would try and direct her from his bed, sometimes just with a hand gesture that suggested that a note needed to be minutely lower. If he moved his fingers, it meant that a phrase needed a little twist or gamak. He would sit up for a few minutes, but spent most of his time lying down, propped up against two well-stuffed bolsters. He was very weak, for his diet had been severely restricted. But over the course of the week, the pallor on his face seemed to have lessened. Dhondutai prayed to the goddess for his recovery and resolved that she would go straight to the temple and sing before her when she returned to Kolhapur.

Baba was managing his father's feet when there was a knock and Shankarrao entered, along with his brother-in-law Ganpatrao.

'Injection time!' he said. Every other evening, he gave his patient a dose of vitamins to get his strength up. The Khansahib willingly lowered his pajamas, without flinching. Although he hated getting poked, this particular doctor had the ability to administer painless injections.

'It's over? Doctor sahib, you are unbelievable!'

'There's a story behind that too, Khansahib!' said Ganpatrao, laughing. 'Did you know that Shankarrao was once a follower of Mahatma Gandhi—though don't ask me why! He would routinely be thrown into prison along with the rest of the freedom fighters. Because he was a trained doctor, he was asked to take care of the sick inmates. He gave so many injections, that through sheer practice, he learned the fine art of stabbing painlessly.'

'Ha ha!' Shankarrao laughed. 'Half the time they didn't even have medicines to cope with the heavy flow of prisoners. They would simply fill injections with saline water and make me administer them to make people feel better. Don't remind me of those days!' he added. 'I have moved from being a socialist to a capitalist now!'

'Yes, but a capitalist with a heart,' interjected Bhurji Khan. They all laughed.

After what seemed to him like two years, rather than two weeks, the Khansahib was allowed to eat regular food. He had been dreaming about this moment. It was only the fear of mortality that had kept him from losing his temper over the restrictions imposed on him. This was the first time in his fifty-odd years that he had gone without meat for more than two days.

But he was going to be in for a serious shock. He had no idea that his milk-fast was only the beginning of a long period of abstinence from all things good. For the next two weeks, his diet would graduate to only boiled spinach and uncooked tomatoes. The doctor had kept him in the dark so that he would be willing to stick out the treatment, one day at a time.

This was a matter of great speculation in the kitchen downstairs on the morning that he was to break his fast.

'How are we going to take this to him? I don't think I have it in me to do it,' said Dhondutai nervously to her aunt, as she chopped the tomatoes into neat little squares.

'There is no doubt he is going to get angry,' she said. 'But there is nothing we can do about it. He has ruined his health with his heavy diet and his smoking. All these Mohammedans eat like this,' said her aunt, shortly. 'It is no surprise our Hindu pandits live so long. What you are is what you eat!'

Dhondutai gasped. In her nervousness over the Khansahib's reaction, she had nicked her finger. She ran to the tap and put her finger under running water.

'Come here, Dhondabai,' said Ishwaramma, an old retainer who had worked with the family for many years. 'Let me bandage that up for you. Don't worry. I will take the food up to your Khansahib. 'He can shout at me if he wants, I don't care. I have encountered worse ogres in my time.'

Precisely at noon, a small procession followed the intrepid Ishwaramma with her tray of flaccid spinach up the stairs to the Khansahib's quarters. Baba was standing at the door, prepared for the worst. Ishwaramma went inside, greeted Bhurji Khan with a 'salaam' and kept the tray in front of him. Ganpatrao went in, sat on the bed opposite the singers, picked up a newspaper, and pretended to read. Dhondutai stood at the door, dreading the first bite.

Sure enough, as soon as Khansahib put a spoonful of spinach in his mouth, he spat it out and bellowed. 'What on earth is this? It is completely tasteless! Where is my real food? What is this nonsense?'

Ganpatrao put his paper down and looked Bhurji Khan straight in the eye. 'Khansahib, you have two choices. Do you wish to live or to die?'

Bhurji Khan's face turned red with rage. But he knew the answer. He ate the rest of the food in silence. Dhondutai watched him and felt terrible. This lion of a man had been brought down so low. What must he be feeling like?

But a month in Hyderabad yielded two important results: Bhurji Khan got better and Dhondutai got five more years of music from him.

Seven

Alladiya Khan died in Bombay a year later, in 1946.

In his last few years, his closest companion was Baba. The old man and his grandson shared a very intimate relationship; it was not constrained by the formal rules of respect and conduct that governed Alladiya Khan's interactions with his sons. Every evening, Baba took him for walks to the beach and they sat on the bench, facing the ocean until the sun dipped into the horizon. Then, before it got too dark, they would walk back. At night, Baba sat by his grandfather's bedside and scribbled down compositions and notations that he murmured to him as and when he remembered them. He slowly chewed his betel leaf, humming old tunes and recalling old memories.

In his last few years, Alladiya Khansahib was teaching Leelabai, the daughter of a close friend and devoted fan, Anantrao Shirgaonkar. She lived five minutes away from Surveyor building. One afternoon, as he sat in front of her, teaching her Shudh Sarang, a melancholic afternoon raga, tears streamed down his face. Leelabai stopped playing the tanpura and said, 'Khansahib. Are you alright? We can stop for a while.'

He simply raised his hand and shook his head. 'No, no, don't stop. I was just remembering the old times. My brother Hyder Khan and I sang this together in the royal court so many times....Where did those times go? And where are those, who were once closest to us now?'

Alladiya Khan did not die in peace. His greatest regret, as he lay suffering on his deathbed, was that his children had not inherited the full worth of his music—one son had been tricked into reclusion, the one who could have become really great died too young, and the third was a fine teacher—he taught Dhondutai as well as other well-known singers—but never had the makings of a performer.

Khansahib was to be buried at a Muslim cemetery off Charni road, near Chowpatty, alongside his long time friend and spiritual mentor, Sayeed Sahib. When a great individual dies, his merit is often measured in terms of the number of people who attend his or her funeral. However, Alladiya Khan's funeral procession was surprisingly spare. There were barely ten or twenty men accompanying the body to the cemetery.

A chronicler of the Khansahib's life asked a Muslim singer, 'When a famous musician dies, you people attend his funeral en masse. How is it that, today, when an emperor of music passed on, none of you cared to put in an appearance?'

The singer replied, with a tinge of sarcasm in his voice, 'Khansahib used to call himself a Hindu Brahmin. We are, after all, low caste Muslims. Why should we attend his funeral?'

Like the great saint-poet Kabir, who called himself neither Hindu, nor Muslim, Khansahib lived—and died— in a no-man's land that few could appreciate. He ate meat, but he also wore the sacred thread of high caste Hindus. He was a follower of Islam, but he composed thoughtful, profound verses that revealed a deep understanding of Hindu philosophy. He did his namaz every day, but sang with complete devotion in temples. He gave the greatest gems of his music to non-Muslim singers. His religion was music.

Dhondutai paused as she tried to remember a composition written by him in Raga Bhairav about Hindu-Muslim unity. She said she would have to search her memory or write to Baba, but would keep it ready for me the next time I came for a lesson.

I forgot about it, but a few weeks later, she handed me an old yellowing envelope, the kind which had its opening flap on the short side. I glanced at her name and address typed out on the front. She was, as usual, mistakenly addressed as 'Mrs Kulkarni.' On the back of the envelope, she had scribbled the first line of the verse:

'Allah, tu karim rahim, sab tero deval aur masjid ...'

Oh god, you are great and merciful. All temples and mosques belong to you. It was an artiste's plea for brotherhood, lost in the cacophony of the times.

Part IV
Kesarbai

One

We sat inside the stuffy room, windows closed to keep out the torrential rain. I was trying to swat a fly which dashed in for shelter and was buzzing around psychotically. Dhondutai watched me and laughed softly. 'Leave the poor thing. Come let's make some tea and relax,' she said. 'What other choice do we have? You can leave when the rain slows down. Until then, why don't we listen to some music recordings?'

'Good idea, baiji.'

We went into her kitchen and I watched the ritual that had intrigued me for the past twenty years. I knew each object so well—the electric lighter she double-clicked to fire up the stove, the rusted green tin filled with aromatic tea leaves, the chipped cup that had faithfully accompanied her from one home to another. She mixed two kinds of tea leaves and left them to steep for a few minutes. 'My tea is like a combination raga. Both individually great tasting, but when melded together just right, what a superb result!'

I smiled. Coming to Dhondutai had become a habit I could not break. I was now married, had moved back to Bombay, and reported on personal finance for *The Times of India*. In between all this, I still took the fast train to Borivli, and continued to weather jokes about my irrational obsession. It was a parallel world that had absolutely no connection with the rest of my life. I found solace in her small universe.

Dhondutai continued to harbor dreams of turning me into a great singer. And I? I tried, but could not devote the time, the unconditional commitment it takes, and kept faltering; missing my lessons because of a late night, one cigarette too many, or a work deadline.

Yet, something had definitely changed for me. I had begun to understand the power of this music. It had entered me. When I sang, I lost myself and my sense of time. My music lesson, and Dhondutai's unconditional love, had become my therapy.

I picked up the cups of steaming tea and proceeded to the music room which had earned its lofty title because it was equipped with a two-in-one cassette player and a cupboard which housed Dhondutai's music, recorded over the years. She gingerly took out a cardboard box containing an assortment of tapes—Sony, TDK, Aiwa—and I picked one out at random. The barely legible writing scrawled across the header read: Dadar-Matunga Cultural Centre, 1976.

I pressed play and a scratchy noise filled the speakers before Dhondutai's voice came on and started to gradually unravel Raga Bihagda. We listened silently for a few minutes. It was a beautiful composition. I softly exclaimed 'wah' every time she completed her cycle with a flourish, and enjoyed her beam at my appreciation.

'Who taught you this, baiji?'

'Kesarbai. It was one of her favorite ragas. In fact, this is what she sang the first time I met her.'

'Tell me about that, please?'

Dhondutai laughed. 'Just listen to the music. That is more relevant!'

'Please, baiji, come on! I'm sure there's a great story there...'

'You are mad! Anyway, if you insist.' She put down her cup and proceeded, in all seriousness. 'I first met her in 1962. The only other time I had seen her was in 1944 at the Vikramaditya Conference. She was performing at the Birla Matoshree Hall near Marine Lines and the three of us bought tickets and went to listen.'

'Who three?'

'Why, my father, me and Baba...'

'Ok, please continue ... Wah!' My attention was momentarily diverted by the music. She had just sung a brilliant passage, playing on the words of the song. I heard exclamations from the audience which had also been recorded. This was the beauty of live performance. Great music was complete only when the notes from the performer touched the soul of the listener and the sigh of appreciation went back to the musician. This connection was like an electric current. In fact, in the days when music was performed in intimate concert halls, the area in front of the stage was usually reserved for what was described as the 'wah-wah group'—listeners who made it a point to respond to the artist with loud approval, sighs and gestures.

The mellow music, this particular raga, the memories that were softly bubbling to the surface, all made Dhondutai warm up to the conversation, and she described her first meeting with the demonic singer who had once guided these notes and taught her how to please the deity inside ga, the dominant swara of Raga Bihagda.

'I think I was about thirty years old, actually a little older,' she started.

'About my age,' I murmured.

'Yes, but unlike you, I was not a foolish dilettante. I took my learning seriously,' she said, with no rancour. I grinned sheepishly, in agreement.

'Yes, so we took the overnight train from Jabalpur to Bombay after Baba read an interview with Kesarbai in a Marathi newspaper where she said that she was finally ready to teach a student who would be worthy of her… '

Baba knew that for Dhondutai to take the music of his gharana forward, Bhurji Khan's training was not enough. He had to introduce Dhondutai to the gharana's most gifted singer. Besides, he could see that his musical sister was languishing in Jabalpur, where she had been living for the last five or six years. Soon after Bhurji Khan died, Dhondutai and her sister had moved to Hyderabad to help their uncle Shankarrao with his ayurvedic company. Seven years later, after a small tiff with the uncle, the whole family moved to Jabalpur where Dhondutai's sister got married, and her brother got his first job. Although she kept up her singing, and gave regular radio concerts, Dhondutai was fading away. Places like Hyderabad and Jabalpur were not musical centres. She needed to be in the big city, beneath the stage lights.

In the fifties and sixties, Birla Matoshree Hall was among the most prestigious auditoriums in the city. Dhondutai, Ganpatrao and Baba walked down the marble stairs, past two enormous busts of the patrons, towards the green room. Father and daughter waited outside while Baba went inside.

There, seated on a chair, with a square halo of glaring bulbs on the mirror behind her, sat Kesarbai. She had the poise of a queen, but sat like a king, her legs slightly apart, her hands on her thighs. She was wearing her signature white silk sari. Large solitaires sparkled in her ears and pearls gleamed on her neck. Seated on the floor around her was her usual coterie—her good friend Shantibhai, her sarangi player Abdul Majid Khan, whose off-white kurta shirt was already bedecked with tiny flecks of crimson betel juice, and Yeshwant Kerkar, who accompanied her on the tabla. These two musicians had loyally accompanied her year after year, and she had taken good care of them so that they did not play with any of her rivals. This was part of her elaborate copyright protection strategy. After all they knew her music more intimately than any one else.

Baba greeted the musicians, touching his hand to his forehead in the customary salute. 'Mai, how are you?' Then he turned to the accompanists. 'Aadaab, Khansahib. Namashkar panditji.'

'Arre, Baba! How good to see you. When did you come from Kolhapur? How is your mother? Come in. Come in.' Kesarbai pulled a comb out of her purse, peered at the mirror, and delicately smoothed her eyebrows.

'Mai, I have brought Dhondutai, Abbaji's student, who had written to you. Would you be agreeable to let her sit behind you on stage today?'

Kesarbai stared at him for a few seconds, with a scalding look that would have burned a hole through one not already familiar with her manner. 'Hmph. Let's see what Bhurji has produced. Bring her in.'

Baba went outside with a grin and told Dhondutai to come in. Father and daughter entered hesitantly. Dhondutai looked at Ganpatrao for approval, touched Kesarbai's feet and stood with her hands clasped together, her gait confident but respectful. Kesarbai looked her up and down. 'So, you think you will be able to accompany me?'

'I'll try, mai. It depends on whether I know the raga you are singing,' Dhondutai replied.

'Of course you know it. I am singing Bihagda. These days, the whole world claims to know Bihagda. Even the low-life bitch who cleans Alladiya Khan's toilets can sing Bihagda. Why won't you be able to sing it?' She guffawed and looked at Majid Khan. 'What do you say, khansahib?' He chuckled back at her. Baba smiled uncomfortably and tried not to look at Ganpatrao to see his reaction.

In one stupendous flourish, Kesarbai confirmed all the rumours about her being an outspoken woman with a filthy tongue. Dhondutai was mortified, but from that moment on, she decided that she would not be distracted by Kesarbai's personality. She was there for only one thing. She would single-mindedly focus on that and ignore the rest.

Later that evening, Kesarbai, sitting between two tanpuras, presented the kind of music that a listener gets to hear only once or twice in a lifetime rendering one extraordinarily beautiful raga after another. Her music had the quality of an uncut diamond. It was raw, sometimes even rough, yet gorgeous. After she finished the last note and the tanpuras stilled, there was a moment of absolute silence before the audience broke into applause. It was clear. No matter how egoistic or ill-mannered she was, when this woman sat down to sing, she was transformed into something higher than her mortal self. Sitting behind her, Dhondutai decided that she desperately wanted a part of this magic.

Kesarbai told Dhondutai to come to Parag, her house in Shivaji Park, the following day. The trio showed up in the evening, carrying the ritual offerings. All of a sudden,

Kesarbai grabbed Dhondutai's hand and brought it closer to her face.

'Who gave you that ring?' she asked the startled Dhondutai.

'A gentleman who heard me sing many years ago.'

Kesarbai stared into space for a few seconds, and then grunted. She looked at the envelope on the tray Dhondutai was carrying, and frowned.

'Please take that back,' she said gruffly.

'Mai, don't embarrass us. This is only a token…'

'No question. If I wanted to make money from teaching I could have made lakhs. What I will be giving you cannot be measured in monetary terms. Don't ever bring up money with me.'

Dhondutai handed the envelope to her father and continued with the ritual, placing a coconut and some flowers on her lap, then garlanding her new teacher. Kesarbai tied a red string around Dhondutai's wrist. This would be the sign that marked the relationship between student and teacher. The string binds and promises loyalty, servitude and, in turn, a life long exchange of music.

After this, Kesarbai's niece brought in a tray of tea and they sat around in awkward silence for a few minutes, while Kesarbai stared at her new student. To Dhondutai's great relief, a few minutes later, Kesarbai's friend Shantibhai walked into the room, breaking the tension. Kesarbai introduced the aspiring singer to him. 'This is the girl Bhurji has taught. She read my interview in *Loksatta*, where I had said I am looking for a singer who has already been trained in this gharana, to take on my legacy. She is a Brahmin girl… from Kolhapur.'

Shantibhai beamed at Dhondutai. He was part of a coterie of wealthy connoisseurs who were deeply devoted to Kesarbai, following her from concert to concert. They spent most of their spare time hanging around her house, listening to her practice, sharing gossip about the music world, and analyzing ragas. People like him, knew her music so well, that once in a while, if she forgot a line while performing, she would turn to one of them—they almost always occupied the front row—and ask what came next. If they proffered the line correctly, she would be grateful, yet irked. While she implicitly trusted them, she was also insanely paranoid about anyone else knowing her music.

This paranoia and suspicion affected her music in many ways. She would often sing a line incorrectly in the composition or throw in some notes in a raga where they shouldn't have been, to mislead any prospective plagiarists lurking in the audience. She had refused to let herself be recorded, turning away the biggest labels of the time. One of the members of the fan club, Babubhai, had surreptitiously been taping her performances—a fact she suspected. So she would periodically barge into his bungalow unannounced, hoping to catch him listening to her music and confiscate all the tapes. But the clever businessman was always one step ahead of her and kept his pirated tape collection well-hidden, usually at Shantibhai's house.

Kesarbai wanted her music to die with her. She wanted listeners to pine for her when she was gone. Shantibhai, Babubhai, and many others, however, couldn't bear the thought of this musical void. Their persistent goading finally convinced her to consider teaching someone and, after much pressure, at the age of seventy, she announced her intentions to teach—though conditionally. When Baba had read the interview in a local newspaper in which she declared, out of the blue, that she was ready to take on a deserving candidate who had already mastered the basics, he had cut it out and sent it to Dhondutai in Jabalpur. She had written to Kesarbai and, to her surprise, heard back. Kesarbai had subsequently invited her to come and see her in Bombay. This was a month ago.

Shantibhai turned to Dhondutai. 'Sing something, my dear.'

Dhondutai looked at her father who nodded encouragingly. She started strumming the tanpura and sang Raga Purvi, systematically laying out the raga the way it had been taught to her by Bhurji Khan. After she finished, she put the tanpura down and looked at Kesarbai expectantly.

'That was good, Bhurji has done a good job. But you need to work on your stylization. You need to individualize the composition, not sing it exactly the way it was taught to you. This is what differentiates the great performers from those who are merely good,' said Kesarbai. She then called out to her sister. 'Let's bring out some sweets. We have a new member in our family.'

They fixed the lessons for five in the evening, Tuesdays and Fridays, and Dhondutai agreed to comply with Kesarbai's conditions: that she would not perform in public venues without her permission, and would not teach anyone. Within two months, Ganpatrao sold his house and land in Kolhapur and bought a flat in Bombay, at Anand Nagar, on Forjett Street. He, Ayi and Dhondutai moved into a small two-room flat, a twenty minute bus ride away from where Kesarbai lived.

When she went back for her first lesson, Dhondutai automatically greeted her teacher by touching her feet. Kesarbai held her shoulders, lifted her gently and said, 'You are a Brahmin's daughter. There is no need for you to do that.' But this was something Dhondutai would not compromise on—even though she knew that she and Kesarbai occupied two ends of a social order in which women were either 'good' or 'bad,' respectable or indecent. These were labels that had been stuck on by men, by society, and Dhondutai would not fall into that trap.

Baba was still in Bombay and came with them for the first few sessions. They all sat around and chatted before starting the lesson. Kesarbai's youngest granddaughter came and stood behind Ganpatrao and stared at the wisp of hair that hung from the back of his head. Within a few weeks she would be pulling at it and running out of the room before her grandmother could catch her.

'You know, I had actually seen you sing about ten years ago,' said Kesarbai to Dhondutai. 'I had been hearing your name as the young protégé of this gharana, and was curious to see what you were all about. So I came to one of your concerts.'

'You did? I don't believe you,' said Dhondutai, laughing shyly. 'Tell me what I was wearing, and what I sang.'

'Oh, I remember clearly. You were in a white silk nine-yard sari with a gold border, and wore your hair in a long plait. You walked onto the stage with great confidence, sat down and, without much ado, started with a perfect sa. You sang Raga Bhoop. It was solid. I remember thinking, Bhurji's done a good job.'

'That's absolutely right, mai. Now I know you aren't just pulling my leg.'

Kesarbai then turned to Baba and said, 'So, young man, how many children do you have now?

He looked sheepish and smiled. 'Er, five, mai.'

'What are you? A flour mill—that you keep grinding them out?' Kesarbai chuckled and her granddaughter suppressed a giggle.

Dhondutai was confounded. Should she laugh at the joke cracked by her new guru? Then, she would insult Baba, who was also like a guru to her. Or, should she stay quiet? But then, Kesarbai may be offended. Dhondutai chose to stare at her toes for a few minutes, while Kesarbai roared with laughter. This would be the kind of maddening dilemma that Dhondutai would have to contend with for the next ten years.

The tape ended with a soft click. Dhondutai touched her ears and shook her head with a shudder. 'You have no idea what used to come out of her mouth. What a woman!' She paused and added, 'Actually, she was more like a man...'

I had heard so much about this intrepid woman who had more enemies than friends. The stories are legendary—like the time she won the Padma Vibhushan. Kesarbai was walking down the steps of the president's office in Delhi, when she ran into Indira Gandhi, who was then Prime Minister of India. They greeted each other respectfully. After exchanging pleasantries, Mrs Gandhi requested Kesarbai to place her hand on her throat. She said that the touch of a great singer would ensure that her voice would always be in good shape. Kesarbai retorted, with a laugh: 'Your voice seems fine, madam. You shout quite a bit already,' and sailed past the stunned Prime Minister.

Another time, she was asked to perform at a programme to celebrate the formation of the state of Maharashtra in 1960. After she sang, Chief Minister Yeshwantrao Chavan went up to her and said, 'Ask for anything and it will be yours.'

'Are you sure,' she said, her eyes twinkling.

'Of course, Kesarbai. Today is a historic day for the city and for the people of Maharashtra. And you have graced the occasion with your tremendous art.'

'Then give me your office for one day.'

The chief minister kept his cool. 'What will you do with it, Kesarbai? Do tell me, and I shall try and implement what you have in mind.'

Kesarbai laughed and said, 'Never mind. But next time, don't make promises you cannot keep!'

When Dhondutai lay down to nap, I went into the other room and stared at the portrait of the woman with the voice of a man; a woman whose temper had once prompted a wealthy Bombay businessman to crawl under the creaky wooden stage and sit in hiding for two hours so that he could listen to her music, because she had banished him from attending her concerts after they had had a tiff.

Kesarbai was known for her tempestuous outbursts in public. She would scrutinize her audience like a hawk and ensure that none of her 'enemies' was present. If someone made the mistake of coughing while she was singing, and she happened to be in a bad mood, she would stop in the middle of her performance and order the hapless listener to leave the auditorium.

Why was she so mean spirited, yet so gifted? So narcissistic and self-destructive? How did these base traits exist in conjunction with her sublime art? Or could it be the other way around? That to achieve that level in music, or any creative endeavour, demands an element of mania? I found, as I entered her world, that Kesarbai's determination to become a great singer—the best in the world—was not a spiritual quest. Rather, it was driven by vengeance, and rooted in unimaginable pain.

Two

It was 1914. A lavish feast was underway. Two well-known Marathi families were joining in matrimony through their children Hirabai and Anantrao. The men strolled into the hall from the front entrance, greeting one another jovially. The women, as was the custom, came in from the back and stayed there, hovering around the bride, commenting on her jewellery, gossiping about the decor. As the men sat around sipping sandalwood sherbet, they were surprised to see a young woman amble in through the front gate. She must have been in her early twenties. She wore a silk sari with a sleeveless blouse. Her eyes were lined with kohl, her lips faintly stained with betel leaf. Her neck glistened with a gold necklace. There was no shawl of modesty wrapped around her shoulders which was customary among women in those days. She didn't pay attention to any one, but was conscious of the eyes on her, some lascivious, others merely curious. She glided jauntily into the women's enclosure. An audible murmur went around the party of men and one of them got up, strode inside and whispered something into his wife's ear. A few minutes later, the groom's mother called the bride's mother aside.

'Who is that woman?'

'Her name is Kesar. She is one of our tenants. She lives in the building across ours.' Hirabai's mother did not dare reveal that the pretty young guest was quite friendly with her daughter. Or, that they would holler and squeal at each other from their windows, even if they were separated by an unbridgeable social chasm.

'Well, clearly, she does not belong here. Women like that should not be at functions like ours. We are Brahmins. What will people say... ' hissed the mother of the groom.

'Tai. What do you want me to do? I can't possibly ask her to leave now that she is here. That would be deeply insulting.'

'It would be far more inauspicious for her to stay. The ceremony is exactly half an hour away. If you still want the wedding to take place, please make sure she is not here. The choice is yours.'

The hostess hurriedly went and whispered something in the young woman's ear. Kesar stared at the older woman in disbelief. Her kohl-lined eyes filled up but she did not allow even a drop to escape. Then, without saying a word, she got up and left.

As she walked home crying in the noonday sun, the enraged young woman swore to herself that one day, she would make this very gentry pine for her.

She did—she became the great Kesarbai Kerkar. But the stigma that surrounded 'singing women' was not about to disappear very quickly. It festered in the hearts of a patriarchal society, which enjoyed its women entertainers but didn't want them mingling with their daughters.

In fact, even fifty years later, people harboured the same feelings about this community. Long after Kesarbai had established herself as a great diva, and long after India had entered an era of so-called modernity, when her granddaughter Ila was getting married in the nineteen seventies, she faced similar murmurs of outrage because of her lineage. It didn't matter that the bride's grandmother was one of the greatest singers India had ever heard. She was, after all, a 'bai,' from the courtesan community.

There are numerous stories about singers like Kesarbai who, despite their artistic achievements, had to silently endure the slights and humiliations flung at them. Gohar Jaan was one of the most formidable women singers of the early nineteen hundreds. She dressed and lived like a queen. She used to wear an invaluable diamond brooch on her left shoulder, which is why she always had two rifle-wielding soldiers stand guard on either side of her while she performed. Once, in Calcutta, she had gone for a ride in a carriage led by four majestic horses. The British governor, who happened to ride past her, automatically saluted her, assuming she was royalty. He was later told that the person in the carriage was a 'singing girl'. He was so livid that he had shown respect to a mere courtesan, that he passed an edict declaring that no one besides royalty could use a four-horse carriage.

The fact that Gohar Jaan was the reigning queen of music in India was not pertinent to her social status, especially in the eyes of men. They may have plied her with pearls and promises in their weak moments, but at the end of the day, she was deemed a woman of disrepute. This was the paradox most women singers lived with.

Like most women singers in her time, Kesarbai came from a community of devadasis. This literally translates into, 'servant of god.'

Devadasis were India's version of the Japanese geisha, women who were trained in the fine art of entertaining wealthy men—sometimes of their choice, but not always. There was a peculiar religious caveat thrown into the equation. Traditionally, these women had to be available for the pleasure of priests and were considered the property of the temple. And because the temples used to be the primary domains for classical music and dance, the women learned to excel in the performing arts. Almost all the great singers and dancers in the early twentieth century had a devadasi lineage.

Society's attitude towards these women was ambivalent and rife with double standards. While they were viewed as 'working women,' they were also perceived as incarnations of a goddess.

Over the years, with Muslim dynasties taking over much of India, the arts moved out of the temples. Music and dance became a mode of entertainment rather than a religious ritual. These women also moved on and became courtesan performers—first in the royal courts, and later in the homes of the landed gentry.

By the eighteenth century, the courtesan singers had popularised a new genre of music, essentially derived from the traditional khayal, but with a lighter, more decorative, edge. It was the thumri, a languid, sensual style. Most compositions were written as odes to love and longing. The style became extremely popular among kings and feudal lords and fit well into the general atmosphere of princely indolence. Singers changed from temple performers to entertainers who relied on wealthy male patrons for support. For this reason, women performers had an edge over male performers, regardless of their talent. There was a time when a number of male musicians were forced to rely on women for sustenance. Men became teachers; women performed.

Given the association of women and the performing arts, the notion of a 'respectable' or virtuous girl singing in public, or even learning music, was anathema. A well-known thumri singer from north India who was not from a professional singer's family but, rather, the daughter of a barrister, had created a completely parallel identity for herself as a singer, which had very little to do with her domestic persona. She would secretly go out and sing on radio under her assumed name. Although she won great acclaim, she could not really enjoy her success. There was always a part of her that wanted to be recognized as a professional and she was thrilled when she was invited to participate in a courtesans conference. It was deeply ironic: she envied their freedom, and they craved what she had by default of birth—respectability.

One of the few times that Dhondutai got angry with me was when I asked her to teach me a thumri. She said, 'Why have you come to me? That's not what I do? If you want to sing thumris, go to some bai.'

Dhondutai had stopped singing thumris ever since the time when, at a private performance in Delhi, a man in the audience had thrown a scented floral string towards her and slurred, 'Please sing a thumri…' She was horrified. She had spent her entire life perfecting the slow, resonant, disciplined khayal. She was a spokesperson for a great classical gharana, and in one swift stroke, some drunk dimwit was trying to take all this away from her and turn her into a mere singing girl in a salon. After that, she decided to remain rigidly, and stoically, opposed to any form of light, entertaining music.

Some purists suggest that the music sung by these professional women is tainted and has defected from the 'sacred' music of the past. But a thumri singer once countered that even though the song is filled with erotic innuendos, the inherent musicality is inspired by the artist's spiritual quest.

For the longest time, my impressions of the courtesan-musician were limited to stories and old black-and-white films. Then, I learned that I too was a part of that world, even if three times removed. The revelation came to me one November evening in a home in west Los Angeles. My husband and I were having dinner with a couple— Dan was an ethnomusicologist and Arundhati a documentary film-maker who was researching the lives of courtesan singers in India.

Over dinner, Arundhati described the strange world of the aging courtesans she had met. 'They were not exactly prostitutes,' she explained. 'And the funniest is that in the olden days, when they worked in the temples, the wives of their patrons would actually pray to them once a year and ask them to take care of their husbands.'

My husband responded with a laugh. 'Not a bad deal, eh? Having my wife hang out with my girlfriend and both praying to take care of me!'

'Perhaps it was a gracious way of institutionalizing infidelity,' I suggested softly. 'But one wonders how all this fits. Were the courtesans happy? Were the wives happy?'

'In some ways, these women were almost envied by the wives, who were not educated, and not exposed to the arts. They did not have the wherewithal to satisfy their worldly husbands' needs,' Arundhati explained. 'One had status and respect in society, the other had the husband's attentions. Sometimes, a professional woman had the option of becoming the wife. In fact, some gave up their art and settled down with a single patron. They bore his children and ran a second household for him. They gave up public performance and within two generations, their children were doctors and lawyers like any other respectable family.'

'And then there was my teacher Dhondutai,' I said. 'She was not born into a family of professional women singers, and had all the opportunity in the world to get married to a suitable boy, but she opted to be alone, just so she could pursue her art, without worrying about husbands and children.'

The conversation veered towards the music world and how I had found my way into it. Although there are no performers in my family, I told them, my great-grandfather had been one of the most generous patrons of music in his time.

'Really? What is his name?' asked Arundhati.

'Lala Shankarlal,' I told her.

She stared at me for a few moments. 'And so you are related to Sir Shriram... Do you remember any thing about so-and-so... ' She named a grand uncle whose name I had vaguely heard of.

It turned out that one of the courtesan singers Arundhati had extensively interviewed, just before she died at the age of ninety, happened to be the long-term mistress of this granduncle. Her name was Mushtari Begum. They had traveled together and he had been a great promoter of her music and poetry. She had even had his children. Somewhere in the heart of old Delhi, there may exist a line of cousins I will never know.

'My research on this subject had to stop because Mushtari Begum's grandchildren were uncomfortable about raking up their lineage. They had acquired respectability, had decent jobs and lives, and preferred to leave it at that,' said Arundhati. 'I beg you, my dear, go find some old retainer in the Delhi family house who can give you more details about the parallel life lived by your grand uncle. This is a story that has to be told because there were so many like him. It is a whole chapter in India's social history that has never been properly documented, only discussed in whispers behind closed doors.'

I later made a few enquiries among surviving relatives. I got nothing out of then. Although not a secret, it was the kind of information that the family didn't particularly like to dwell on. It existed, but was better left unspoken.

I finally happened to meet one uncle who confirmed that Mushtari Begum had, in fact, caused the family great anguish. She used to live in Lyallpur, renamed Faisalabad, where my grand uncle had been sent to look after a textile mill. His involvement with the singer had eventually grown beyond the accepted norms—which tolerated habitual hedonism but not bigamous commitment.

While relating this story my uncle had paused for dramatic effect. 'Now you know that in those days, a man's turban was a sign of his pride and position.' I looked at him quizzically. 'Well, things grew so intense with Mush-tari Begum that your grand uncle's father, one of the most prominent citizens of Delhi, made a trip to Lyallpur, and actually laid his turban down in front of Mushtari Begum with a plea that she leave his son forever.'

And so she did.

Like Mushtari Begum, most women enjoyed a brief burst of popularity in local circles, while they were still young, attractive, and performance-worthy. Most of them sang enough to be able to please their patrons and his friends. Some among them broke out and became legends in their time. But regardless of their talent and fame, they almost always died alone and often impoverished, because their patrons were long gone and they were left to the mercy of children who had spent too many years growing sluggish under the shadow of a working mother.

Three

'You must go and meet Kesarbai's daughter, Sumantai. She is a very good person. She lives with her daughter, Ila,' Dhondutai said to me. Then, her eyes suddenly brimmed over. 'Kesarbai should have stayed with her. Sumantai's only mistake was that she had been born a girl.'

Dhondutai refused to disclose more about the strange relationship between Kesarbai and her daughter. How did Suman end up being the antithesis of her mother? Why did Kesarbai abandon her in her later years? There is very little documented about Kesarbai's personal life. These were not matters to be discussed in public, and certainly didn't find pride of place in hagiographic memoirs.

I decided to visit Parag, Kesarbai's home in Shivaji Park, a three-storey bungalow by the sea not too far from Manjutai's house. I had to understand what it was that made it taboo for Dhondutai and her father to go there after dark. I wanted to smell the shallow-fried fish and sol curry that Kesarbai had relished every single day, and to discover the chameli tree from which she had picked little white flowers every morning and made tiny garlands, to lay before her goddess or to pin onto her granddaughter's hair.

The bungalow stood amidst other similar-looking houses on a quiet lane bordered with trees, off the main road. A few minutes away on the western side was the ocean. For some reason, this area had not been mowed down and transformed into a mess of badly-designed high-rises. There was still an old world charm to it.

I got there at noon and stood for a moment outside the gate, where many early morning walkers had once stopped short in their tracks to listen to the great singer on the third floor as she unfolded her morning raga. I climbed up the stairs that had once borne the footsteps of aspirants and impresarios, tiptoeing up tentatively, only to be rejected and sent scurrying back down. I looked around for some sign, any sign, that one of the greatest singers of India had once lived here. All I saw were unknown name-plates and bolted doors and the damp imprint of rain on old plaster.

I rang the bell. A tall woman with Kesarbai's bright eyes opened the door and warmly welcomed me. 'I am Ila, Kesarbai's granddaughter. Do come in. My mother is waiting for you,' she said.

The room was stark and barely furnished. Inside a pale wizened woman lay on a bed, her back to the wall. She wore a loose fitting gown dotted with faded black paisleys. She slowly got up protesting, with a warm laugh, when I touched her feet. 'Don't make me give away my blessings, I need them for myself.'

Despite the ninety-year-old lines on her face, and a hunch which prevented her from sitting up for too long, there was a muted elegance about her. I looked at her carefully, trying not to stare. This was the baby whom Kesarbai had carried on one knee while she balanced the tanpura on the other, repeating a set of notes till she got it just right, trying desperately to push out of her mind the fact that her child had a fever and must be taken to a doctor. This was the little girl whose hair had been pulled into tight oily plaits so that she looked like a girl from a 'good' family, and not a singing woman's illegitimate child.

When Suman was born, the young Kesarbai was determined to make her daughter the opposite of what she was. Suman was kept far away from the all-night performances. She was sent to a good school down the road with little Parsi girls her age. She was escorted to and from school by a maid at all times. And when Suman passed the crucial exam that qualified her to become a doctor, it was one of the happiest moments in Kesarbai's life. She had changed her destiny. Now, no one could say anything about her past. Yet, the world was weighed heavily against her, and when the lovely and talented Suman married a young doctor from Surat, his family disowned him because of his mother-in-law's profession. It didn't matter that the girl was far wealthier than them or that, when her father Seth Gopaldas was still alive, she had been waited on by servants—a luxury they had never been able to afford their own children. It didn't even matter that she was one of the few women doctors of her time, nor that she was deeply devoted to her husband. Their vision was blinkered by the fact that she was the daughter of a singing woman. And their son had gone against their wishes.

'How is Dhondutai?' Suman asked, her voice tremulous.

'She sends you her best.' There was a long pause and I didn't dare break the silence.

'I'm afraid I don't remember much,' said Sumantai, looking into the distance. 'That is one of the few benefits of old age,' she added with a smile.

'I've come only to meet you. You don't have to trouble yourself,' I responded softly.

We sat there quietly for a few minutes, listening to a cuckoo strain to reach a note higher than the previous one it had struck. Outside the window, a mango tree was resplendently green. I commented that the neighbourhood was almost as green as it must have been when Kesarbai was alive.

'My grandmother loved plants, especially flowering plants' said Ila. 'That was one of her passions. She looked after them herself. And every morning, after her practice session, she would go down and tenderly pluck the flowers to take back up and string into little garlands. She would place these before her gods, or give them to us and we'd clip them on our hair. If she saw people stealing her flowers, she'd get so angry that she'd sometimes throw a bucket of water or even stones at them from her balcony and dare them to come upstairs.'

'That's because they'd break the whole branch in their hurry to get the flower,' Sumantai interjected. 'When someone steals something, they don't value it, so they're not particularly careful how they handle it.'

'Hmm. Perhaps that is how she felt about her music,' I murmured.

'Absolutely,' said Ila. 'You must have heard all those stories about how she didn't like people stealing her music. Well, let me tell you why. If you have nurtured something for many years and built it up to such heights, you do become possessive about it. Then, when people start stealing it from right under your nose, naturally you would get livid. Her music was her wealth. That is all. Don't you lock up your jewellery in a safe and bring it out only for special occasions or people?' asked Ila. 'This was her life. It was not something she felt like distributing for free.'

'Like her flowers, her music was reserved for God and for special people. The rest of the world could go to hell, as far as she was concerned.' I suggested. 'Or they could try and catch the fragrance from a distance.'

Sumantai looked sad and lay down again. She said, 'People misunderstood her. She didn't have an easy life. That's why…'

I held my breath. I didn't wish to probe, but I was desperate for her to continue. I had heard somewhere that when Kesarbai was five or six years old, her maternal uncles discovered that she had a lovely voice. Whenever there were temple festivities in the little Goan village where she was born, she would be made to stay up late into the night and sing. I had visions of a fair little girl, her hair braided tight with red ribbons, falling asleep sitting cross-legged, and being nudged awake at some unearthly hour to go and sing in front of a roomful of strangers.

'She must have had some horrible experiences as a young woman that made her develop such a temper…' I softly prompted, hoping to trigger off some memory that would take me into a world of sepia.

But we lapsed into silence again and went back to listening to the cuckoo's plaintive cry. I had to be patient. These were not stories that came spilling out of people's homes easily. There was too much to run away from, and a selective memory, reinforced over the years, was far easier to fall back on.

'Tell her the story of that time you were late from school…' said Ila, trying to be helpful.

'Oh yes. I must have been ten or eleven,' said Sumantai, as if waking from her reverie. 'She was very protective of me. Even when I was a little girl, I was not allowed to step

221

out of the house to play. I went everywhere with a female escort. I would be home every evening at ten minutes after five after school. One day, I didn't come straight home, but went to a friend's house to see some cherry flowers because she used to wear them in her hair and I really loved them. She invited me to come and see the tree from which she plucked them. By the time I reached home, it was after five-thirty. My mother was sitting there, staring at the clock, poised like a tigress waiting for her prey. In this case, the victim of her wrath was the poor lady who came to pick me up from school, whom I had bullied into accompanying me to my friend's house. She screamed at her for disobeying her instructions and not bringing me straight home. After that day, I never strayed. I just went to school and came back. I did my studies. I hardly had any friends. They could only be children whose parents Kesarbai had met. And as you know, she didn't meet such people much.'

'Yes, she was very strict, even with us, her grand-daughters,' said Ila. 'Our skirts always had to be below our knees. If we went out to play, we had to be back by a certain time. And definitely before it became dark.'

'The funniest thing was that she never really let us close to her music,' said Sumantai. Her eyebrows went up and she looked surprised, as if she was thinking about this for the first time. 'Her single-minded ambition was to make me a doctor—and a lady.'

'You mean you don't sing at all? This tradition stopped with you?'

'No, I don't sing. I can barely recognize one raga from another,' she said, smiling.

Sumantai looked at her feet. I noticed that they were almost translucent, webbed with pale green veins. 'I think she just didn't want me to go through the things she went through,' she paused. 'She went out of her way to make sure that we would never be a part of her world.'

Dhondutai had once told me about an encounter Kesarbai had in Patiala, a wealthy kingdom in north India, which became famous for the king-size whisky peg ordered by its decadent rulers. Before Kesarbai became a student of Alladiya Khan, she used to learn music from a famous sitar player, Barkatullah Khan. He was employed by the Patiala king as court musician. He invited his protégé, Kesarbai, to come there and participate in a musical jamboree.

The music hall was vast, with plush velvet-lined chairs along the walls. The singers were seated on floor cushions on one side of the hall. On the other side, on raised sofas sat the princes and their courtiers. One of the princes had two women dressed gorgeously, standing on either side of him. One woman whispered something into his ear. The next thing Kesarbai knew, a burly turbaned servant showed up by her side and told her the prince was calling her to sit next to him. Kesarbai retorted, 'I have come here to sing, not sit with the prince.'

This was reported back to the prince, who promptly sent the servant back to Kesarbai and demanded that his orders be followed. The battle cry had been declared. Kesarbai looked at the man and said, 'There is no way I am going there.' Suddenly, he grabbed her arm and started to drag her along. In the scuffle that followed, her necklace broke and a spray of milky white pearls went flying across the room. She pulled away and landed on another courtier, who whispered into her ear, 'Don't worry, you are safe with me.' He then turned to the prince and said, 'Since she has fallen on my lap, she is mine.'

'It was only at that moment that Kesarbai's heart started beating at its regular pace again,' said Dhondutai.

But the courtier was not able to rescue her from the decadent ruler. The king did not permit Kesarbai to leave the state of Patiala for almost six months. Letters were kept away from her and she was not allowed to send messages home. In this gilded prison, she had no rights or recourse. Finally, the court musician Barkatullah Khan, who had brought her there in the first place, managed to convince the king to let her go. This was when she returned to Bombay.

While the story may have been embellished or edited, this sort of thing could easily have taken place and probably did, not once but several times—to Kesarbai, or her mother, or aunt or friend, leaving, like the sediment the waves leave behind to create a craggy cliffside, layer after layer of rage.

Dhondutai shook her head. 'Things were not easy for these women. No wonder she educated her daughters and nieces and led them towards respectability. I clearly remember one evening, when I had gone there for my lesson, Kesarbai's young grand niece was sobbing in the room. I asked her what was wrong, and she said that she had just been standing in the balcony and looking out on to the street. Suddenly, Mai had yelled at her and told her never to stand there once the sun had set. 'What did I do wrong? I don't understand why she lost her temper like that,' the little girl said.

'My heart went out to her,' said Dhondutai. 'How on

earth was I to explain to her that the reason she had not been allowed to stand at the balcony in the twilight was because that was where certain types of women stood when they wanted to attract customers. Under no circumstances, should she be mistaken for being one of them. Mai had seen to it that that sordid chapter would be over for this family.'

Four

In the 1920s Bombay, the city by the sea, was home to a new breed of maharajas. They were the textile barons who had grown rich off a system where cotton was being grown and spun into yarn in India, and sent to the mills of Manchester, where it would be woven into cloth and shipped back to India. The mill owners of Bombay were captive suppliers. There was very little for them to do; the yarn kept spinning and the money kept rolling in. Since they had all the time in the world, they could afford to indulge in other pleasures, like music and dance. In fact, these businessmen became the reason music stayed alive after princely patronage faded out.

It became a status symbol for a wealthy man to support a woman singer who may also have been his lover. But this equation did not fit into the traditional paradigm of rich man and exploited mistress. Rather, there was mutual respect. The children she bore from her patron would be fully provided for, though they would stay with her and keep her name. There was an unspoken understanding that she or her family would not in any way interfere with, nor challenge, the patron's legal family. A social order was thus maintained and the patron would continue to preside at the dinner table with his wife and children sitting around him, as if absolutely nothing were amiss. If he was away three nights a week, no one questioned his absence. The wife learned to freeze her heart until the time when she could unleash her frustrations—on a daughter-in-law or a servant, or by means of a prolonged illness.

The long white cushions had been laid out. The gas lamps were lit and jasmine garlands had been hung along the windows so that they could catch the breeze. The guests began to arrive in horse-driven carriages. The rustle of silk and the aroma of perfume filled the room.

A wealthy music lover from Calcutta was visiting Bombay. In his honor, someone had arranged a three-day music concert for a select gathering, in a private home somewhere in Santa Cruz. Tarabai Shirodkar, one of the great singers of that time was to perform and, before her, a young upcoming singer called Kesarbai.

A carriage pulled by two splendid white horses arrived at the bungalow. The doorman opened the door and a buxom woman in her late twenties wearing a blue chanderi sari with a sleeveless blouse, stepped out. Pearls and diamonds sparkled on her neck and the aquamarine pendant matched her sari perfectly. Her hair was up in a bun and around it was a halo of white flowers. Her nails were short and painted a startling crimson. The host standing at the door said, 'Greetings, Kesarbai.'

Tarabai had seen to it that Kesarbai would sing first. Indian musicians are very particular about who sings before and after them—not just because of egos and hierarchies, but also because it affects the performance.

These women occupied a strange world. On the one hand they helped each other. At the same time, they were competing for the same small group of clients. There was underlying empathy and yet they knew they had to be the prettier woman, the better singer, the more passionate lover. It was only the handful who became great artistes who could live without the lovers and patrons. The others had no choice.

Kesarbai's performance was not up to the mark. She was not familiar with her tabla accompanist, and was nervous in front of the audience of powerful, wealthy connoisseurs. Tarabai came on next, and lifted everyone's spirits. In the middle of performing she said, half-joking, 'At least my notes will dispel the discordant notes left in the atmosphere by Kesarbai.' The audience tittered.

The evening became a turning point for Kesarbai and the history of Indian classical music.

Outraged by the public insult she went home and cried for hours. She made up her mind that an incident like this would never happen again. She would do whatever it took to become the greatest singer in the country. There would be none like Kesarbai for the next hundred years. She would show them all. She had been wandering around trying to learn music from too many singers without getting any real training. Now she needed the best teacher there was. She had to have the voice culture that would make her aalaaps resound through the auditorium; she had to get the secret of the two-note taan which would send her vocal chords flying; she wanted the beautiful compositions that would make her immortal. There was only one man who could help her achieve all this. His name was Alladiya Khan.

Kesarbai's chief patron at the time was Seth Gopaldas. He gently tried to tell her that Alladiya Khan might not agree to teach her. He was known to look down on professional bais. He already had his sons. Why would he waste his time teaching a woman? Besides, he had taught Kesarbai briefly and unsuccessfully eight years ago.

But she had made up her mind and nothing would change that. Finally, Gopaldas knew that he had to do something. There was no hope in trying to suppress a volcano. He came up with a ruse. It just so happened that his close friend, Vithaldas, knew Alladiya Khan quite well. He got him to write to the court singer of Kolhapur. A telegram was sent out. It said: 'Vithaldas is dying. Proceed to Bombay immediately.'

The Khansahib arrived. When he walked into the house, he was shocked to see his friend calmly reclining on a swing, sipping sherbet, instead of lying, as he had imagined him, feverishly in bed.

'What on earth? You lied to me…' he said, in an unusual fit of anger.

'Calm down, Khansahib. Calm down. Let me explain everything to you…'

He sat him down. A few minutes later, Gopaldas arrived, in accordance with the plan, and sat with them. Vithaldas then took the plunge. 'Khansahib, we would really like you to take on Kesar as a student and give her every thing you have.'

Alladiya Khan appeared stunned and did not say anything. The two friends waited patiently in silence. After a long pause, he said, 'Vithaldas, you have put me in a real quandary by placing such a request before me. I don't know if you know this, but I taught this girl when she was nineteen or twenty years old for a few months. She wasn't able to learn my kind of music so I stopped. I later heard that she had gone around saying that I don't know how to teach. Although over the last couple of months, I have been hearing that she wants to learn from me again, I don't think I want to teach her...'

Gopaldas and Vithaldas gave each other knowing looks but didn't say anything.

'I have another issue,' Alladiya Khan continued. 'I am currently employed with Shahu Maharaj in Kolhapur and he takes care of me and my family's needs. I can't really afford to leave that job.'

'The Kesar of eight years ago is very different from the Kesar of today,' Vithaldas cajoled. 'You can hear her yourself and determine that. As for her spreading that vile rumour about you, I can assure you that it is untrue and someone has been filling your ears. Finally, if you are worried about leaving the king, all that has been taken care of. I have requested the maharaja through a friend to let you go. Gopaldas here has agreed to take on all your expenses and you will have no problem whatsoever.'

Alladiya Khan once again lapsed into meditative mode. The room swelled with silence. Then he said slowly, 'I have one final issue. My music is highly sophisticated. I confess I don't feel entirely comfortable teaching this music to a woman of her community, if you know what I mean.' The Khansahib had even heard rumours about a liaison between Kesarbai and his own son, Manji Khan. A shadow crossed his face when the thought came to him.

Vithaldas had anticipated this and he was quick to respond. Hadn't the Khansahib once taught a young stage actress who used to be patronized by a wealthy individual in the town of Sardar? He didn't mention it, but there had been some sort of relationship between the Khansahib and actress as well. No one could throw stones. He simply said, 'But you taught Malubai.'

Still hoping to dodge the pressure of this job that had landed before him, the Khansahib conjured up a draconian set of conditions: A sum of five thousand rupees would be paid at the outset; and two hundred rupees plus any additional expenses, would be paid every month. This would go to him even if some natural cause prevented the tuitions from taking place; she would have to learn from him for at least ten years; and if he had to travel to other places, she would accompany him there.

All terms were accepted—and the official student-teacher initiation ceremony took place on January 1, 1921. Thus began one of the greatest musical partnerships of the twentieth century.

A few nights later, Gopaldas was over at Kesarbai's house. They lay in bed together and discussed this great new development in her life. It was quiet, except for the distant sound of the sea lapping gently against the city. The bed creaked as Gopaldas turned on his side to face his lover, resting his head on his elbow.

'Kesar,' he said, gently.

'Yes, Seth?' She looked at her benefactor and smiled.

'You know what the Khansahib has said, don't you?'

'Yes, that I must not have any more children if I wish to learn under him.'

'That means we must not meet like this any more,' he whispered to her. 'We will continue to be good friends and you will always be my confidante.'

'Yes, Seth.'

'We cannot let our needs come in the way of your musical training. This is a turning point in your life. You are now not just a singing bai but a young woman with a great career ahead of you, and it is not to be taken lightly. Do whatever it takes to become the best, my girl. You must shine forth. May God be with you.'

With that, the much older man who had fathered Kesarbai's only daughter and taken care of her every need, walked out of her life as her lover. He, however, continued to provide for her and saw to it that his daughter, Suman, had everything she could want.

After a brief period of celibacy, it is rumoured that Kesarbai continued to have many lovers—sometimes several at a time.

Alladiya Khan and Kesarbai had a profoundly ambivalent relationship. It was not premised on the idealised notions of the student-teacher relationship. The lessons were driven by desperate and worldly desires—she wanted to become the greatest singer in the world, and he needed the money. He knew that after the death of Shahu Maharaj, his value in the court of Kolhapur would diminish. The young princes were more inspired by fast horses than sombre ragas. Vithaldas' offer came right about the time he needed it most.

They didn't pretend to care about each other. Yet, both student and teacher were bound by the sense of duty—to learn and to teach—and their music transcended all else.

There was a period when the training became extremely intense, and went from morning until late into the night. But there was a small problem. Kesarbai had a neighbour whose sons were in various stages of school and college.

Their studies were being affected by the persistent singing that came from the bungalow next door. When Alladiya Khan was told about this, he pointed out that Kesar was just picking up the nuances of the style and it was not a good time for them to stop their training. So, he arranged for them to move to Sangli, a quiet town south of Bombay. He asked Kesarbai's brother Baburao to rent a small house in an open field so that no one would get disturbed. Kesarbai, her sister-in-law, and the Khansahib moved there. This was where he taught her the secrets of the gharana and how to unfold and showcase a raga. Here, she learned Raga Bihagda and four or five other ragas. The four months were one of the most critical phases in her musical training. The Khansahib turned her into a concert singer.

Within ten years, Kesarbai became one of the highest paid singers of her time. Whether or not people understood her music, being seen at her concerts became a sign of cultural arrival, even a fashion statement.

A few years before Alladiya Khan died, he gave one of his last private concerts in Bombay. Kesarbai had long stopped learning from him, but came to listen. He presented some rare ragas, including Sampoorna Malkauns, an unusual version of the otherwise popular raga, Malkauns. Sampoorna means complete, which meant that the raga featured all seven notes of the scale. Kesarbai was mesmerized by her teacher's rendering, for at this late age, his music was filled with a lifetime of experiences and had been honed to near perfection. But she was also angry because he had not taught her this raga.

The very next morning her carriage pulled up outside Alladiya Khan's flat in Surveyor building. She sauntered in and said, with a frown, 'Khansahib, why didn't you teach me this one?'

Baba was there, pressing his grandfather's feet. He looked up at the aged man who was, as usual, deep in thought, flicking his rosary beads. The Khansahib said, 'I have so much to give. Is it my fault that no one has emptied my stomach of everything?'

'Please. I wish to learn it.' Her voice was softer this time.

Baba gently pointed out that the Khansahib was too old to travel all the way to Shivaji Park where she now lived. Kesarbai said she would arrange for their lessons to take place down the road from the Khansahibs' place in Babulnath, at the tabla player Vishnu Shirodkar's home on Laburnum road. For the next two months, both Kesarbai and Alladiya Khan showed up diligently every morning and Kesarbai, learned her last raga: Sampoorna Malkauns. She also made him teach her how to sing a bol-taan, because she had heard her arch rival sing one. At the time, the Khansahib was around ninety and Kesarbai was close to fifty.

'This was also the time I learned this raga, while listening to their lessons,' Baba later told me. 'And I was able to teach it to Dhondutai.' We were sitting in Baba's house in Kolhapur, almost sixty years after the death of his grandfather. He reached out to a book lying next to his bed and flipped it open. 'In fact, I want you to carry to her a short verse I have composed in the raga, the fast dhrut tempo piece that comes after the main composition. She asked me to teach it to her a few years ago.' He then recited his composition, signed off with his pen name Ahmad Das, which meant the servant of Ahmad. Ahmad was the name used in compositions by his grandfather, Alladiya Khan.

Five

'Did you know that Kesarbai's music is circulating through the solar system?' said Dhondutai, peering at me through her reading glasses. She was writing a speech for a Kesarbai memorial concert, where she had been asked to speak on the greatness of her guru. I gave my teacher a bemused look, but suspended disbelief for the story that would follow, for I knew it would be charming, even if apocryphal.

Many years ago, an American space scientist decided to send a time capsule into orbit. The idea was that if ever planet Earth were to get destroyed in some galactic outburst, some memory of it would be saved. The capsule contained random objects including a sheet with mathematical principles, photographs of famous monuments, art works, and—as far as this story is concerned—some music recordings.

Now, this scientist had once heard a haunting recording of Kesarbai Kerkar's Bhairavi and wanted it to be included in the capsule. He deputed his assistant to source that recording. No one seemed to know where to find it. Everyone insisted that there were no published recordings available because she had not allowed it. Finally, after scouring music libraries and stores, the assistant chanced upon a dusty hole-in-the-wall Indian store in New York.

She found a sleepy man behind the counter, wearing a purple and green checkered shirt.

He disappeared into a back room and brought out a carton, also covered with the same kind of checkered cloth and dumped it on the ground, sending off a cloud of dust. The student sneezed and shrank back, then knelt down and started sifting through the box. It contained stacks of old shellac records. The covers of some of the 78 RPMs crumbled in her hands and she sneezed again. Finally, amidst the dust and scurrying spiders, she saw a picture of a lovely woman, with her hair parted on the side, and a string of pearls around her neck. Underneath, it announced: Bai Kesarbai Kerkar. It was an HMV record. The assistant pulled it out and wiped it with the checkered cloth. She was in luck. It featured Kesarbai's searing Bhairavi.

The woman asked the shop owner how much she should pay him. He mumbled a ridiculously low price. She pressed double the amount into his palm and ran out of the store, clutching a smiling Kesarbai in the crook of her arm.

Ironically, it was because of this very record label that Kesarbai had developed her passionate disapproval of recording, and banished all record companies from her life. Around the 1930s, this Madras-based company had bought the rights for producing gramophone records from a British company. The shellac records were manufactured by the Crystalate Gramophone Record Manufacturing Company in London. The company had published several hundred titles of vocal and instrumental music from all over India. Kesarbai's was one of them.

However, the company was suddenly dissolved and the excess stock was disposed of with utter disregard for its value. Someone came back and reported to Kesarbai that they had found her record being sold on a pavement for a quarter of its original price. She was aghast. How could the reigning queen of music, who only traveled in a horse-carriage or chauffered car, lie on a pavement? For her, it was akin to selling oneself on the streets. Or, disposing of valuable jewels from the family treasury for one hundredth of their value. She decided that she would never allow her music to be compromised again. It took years before she succumbed to His Masters' Voice and sang the scintillating three minute gems that her fans cherish to this day. Of course, even there, she hedged by muffling a few words here and there, so that no one could use her recording to copy her.

Kesarbai's antagonism towards recording companies was not unusual, at least in the early days of the electronic revolution. Most artistes feared technology—not just recording studios, but also the microphones and wires that had started encroaching on stage—because it represented the unknown. Their voices didn't sound the way they used to. The famous Bade Ghulam Ali Khan actually believed that the recording equipment pulled life out of the voice, leaving an artist insipid and impotent, a notion worse than death for the robust, meat-eating singer from Punjab. He had once, reportedly, run out from an All India Radio recording studio in Delhi on the pretext that he couldn't handle the smell of the paint inside the room. The truth was that this otherwise famously outspoken man was utterly scared!

Kesarbai too detested the intrusion of mikes on stage, because they distracted her, especially when they crackled in the middle of her singing. She viewed the microphone as a barrier between herself and the audience. Her stentorian voice had been trained to reach the last row in the hall, she didn't need these wires and steel contraptions.

There were deeper reasons why these musicians were leery of being recorded. Unlike western compositions, which are written scores, open to some degree of interpretation but essentially fixed structures, Indian classical music is fluid and amorphous and as hard to contain as the ocean's waves. A raga will never be rendered exactly the same twice over, even if sung or played by the same musician. There are so many variables that influence its expression; the artiste's mood, the audience's response. The music played inside a recording studio may be more self-conscious, more stultified, than the music played before a group of enlightened connoisseurs. And the tenor of the music would again change if it were being performed in a temple.

Kesarbai often broke into conversation with her friends in the middle of a concert… 'So, Shantibhai, what did you think of that re I just struck?' and she would get the appropriate reactions from her fan club. Some of her spontaneous interruptions feature in the secret recordings that were made unbeknownst to her, and although crude, they add a tremendous flavor to the listening experience and bring her alive, fleetingly, even fifty years later.

Dhondutai once recounted the time when she herself was being recorded by a Bombay label. She chose to sing Raga Desh, followed by Malhar. After the session, the team listened to the replay. While Desh worked out to her liking, Dhondutai was not satisfied with her Malhar. Something was missing. It was hard to put a finger on it. She was going to let it pass, but her worldly-wise student Vasant, who was with her at the time, warned her that once imprinted on vinyl, there was no going back. He urged her to re-record it, and the music director was thrilled when she agreed. She took a short break, her tabla accompanist Padhye Master went outside for a smoke, and then they sat down for the second take.

After she finished, the music director, an elderly man called Abbas, came up to her and said, 'Dhondutai, that was electrifying. But I can't understand how it was so different. The whole raga seemed to be lifted on to a higher scale and had a newfound vibrancy.'

She laughed. 'I have no idea what I did earlier. But it is probably because, in the morning, one's voice is a little heavier. By the time the day swings around, and you have sung some, you warm up quite differently. Anyway, I'm glad it all worked out!'

And when Dhondutai sings the same Malhar today, almost twenty years later, it feels completely different. The composition is the same, as are the notes and melody, but there is an emotive quality in the music. She explains it readily. 'I have spent a lifetime meditating on these ragas. That is all I do, in fact. I try and think of ways I can present it better. But more than that, I have lived life, been through its rollercoaster rides, and the emotion that comes through in my music today is a reflection of that.

'I've noticed that when a musician is young, her music contains a boisterous quality. She usually wants to show off. When she grows a little older, the focus is on virtuosity. It is only after forty that you truly begin to become an artiste. Your voice changes, your emotions change and therefore your music is bound to change. That's when the music ages, like a good pickle, and seeps into the musician's entire being.'

This is the reason that a recording is only a small slice of a musician. It can never be remotely representative. Alladiya Khan's biographer, Govindrao Tembe, wrote that a recording is like a photograph. You can see the person's expression, or what he is wearing, at that moment—you will not get an understanding of his complete personality. It was a good thing that Alladiya Khan was never recorded, even if posterity may never get to glimpse his genius. When the technology came to India, he was close to seventy-five and on the decline. If he had been recorded then, his signature would have faltered. It would not have been the real him. In such cases, things are better left to the imagination.

Six

When she agreed to take Dhondutai on as a student, Kesarbai was a mellow seventy-year-old. Her patron had long since passed on and there were no more late night concerts in the house. Kesarbai was now an admired artist who sang only at the top music festivals in the country. Even so, Ganpatrao accompanied Dhondutai to her lessons at Parag because it would be inappropriate to send his daughter to the house of a professional singer alone. Besides, he played an important role—he accompanied his daughter on the tabla.

Ganpatrao had bought a small apartment in Anand Nagar on Forjett Street, at the foot of Cumballa Hill. The Kulkarni family gradually settled into the big city. While Ganpatrao and Dhondutai were excited about their new adventure, the person who was most disturbed about the move was Ayi. She craved to be close to her son and new-born grandson in Jabalpur.

Besides, she was extremely concerned about Dhondutai's future. Her daughter was past thirty. It was all very well that she had decided to pursue music as a career, but did she know what came with the territory? It was a very public and cruel space. How would they fit into this world? Dhondutai must, in no way, compromise her reputation. Music or no music, she was the daughter of a respectable Brahmin.

Ayi wiped her brow as she started taking out the gleaming brass and steel kitchen utensils that had been packed into a trunk, placing them on the solitary shelf in her new kitchen. She remembered the argument she had had with her husband in the darkness, just before they left Jabalpur. The children had been sleeping—or, at least, that is what she thought.

Dhondutai was awake across the room from them, and had listened to the whispers. She sensed her mother's pain and also the heavy will of her father. Both stayed suspended above her like a dark grey chord in a monsoon raga.

By and by, Ayi had no choice but to fall into the routine of big city life. She found out where the nearest vegetable vendor sat and where they could get their wheat grain ground. Ganpatrao figured the best route to take for his early morning walk, which he continued unfailingly, replacing the largesse of Kolhapur's lake with the somewhat more humble tanks and gardens of Bombay. For Dhondutai, the city opened up a whole new world but, above all, she was thrilled to be training under one of the greatest singers of the time.

Ganpatrao knew that his wife was having a difficult time settling in. He tried to make up for it in little ways. Sometimes he would bring home the blue flower which used to grow in her garden in Kolhapur. Or he tried to spend more time at home. But he knew she was lonely and missed her old friends and family who would gather around and gossip with her in the evenings.

'Aaho, you won't believe what happened this morning,' he said, as he entered the door and took off his slippers. His wife looked up from the kitchen where she was grating a coconut. 'I was walking near Chowpatty, and a young man came and threw himself at my feet. He said he used to be a student at the ashram outside Kolhapur and recalled how I used to bring boxes of your home-made sweets to their school and give the orphans a break from their spartan meals.' Ganpatrao added a liberal pinch of white lie to his story. 'He said he will never forget your shrikhand.' Ayi smiled and promised that she would make some in the evening. Ganpatrao went and sat next to his petite wife and put his arms around her. She lay her head on his shoulder and neither of them spoke.

Gradually, amidst the uncaring fast-moving crowds of the city, Ganpatrao discovered more people who had been part of their former world. He started to establish connections with other Brahmins in the Girgaum area, close to where they lived. A number of Kolhapur's Brahmins had moved to Bombay over the years. Some had gravitated towards opportunity, some to try and obliterate the scars of persecution.

One such Brahmin friend, Sapre, was a regular visitor to the Kulkarni home. He was a trained priest. On festival days, he would go to different homes and conduct the rituals that the family could not, or did not know how to, do.

Sometimes he stayed behind and listened to Dhondutai as she practiced, while her father accompanied her on the tabla. If she sang Raga Megh, he would look outside and tell her he saw peacocks dancing on the hill. After she finished he said, 'Daughter, I envy you. I may sit here day after day and offer prayers to these statues, but you have found a shortcut to the gods.'

Dhondutai laughed, but she knew that he was not joking.

Over the next few weeks, Sapre noticed that Ganpatrao was not able to keep up with the long hours that Dhondutai would sing. His left wrist would start aching and his tempo would slow down. Ganpatrao was too committed to his daughter's musical career to admit that this was a problem and refused to acknowledge his pain.

One morning, as they sat together and sipped tea, Sapre said, 'Ganpatrao, I know of a very capable young man who is learning tabla and looking for some work.' There was silence all around, for Sapre was touching on a sensitive area. He continued. 'He lives three doors down from me in my chawl. If you like, you can try him out. I can vouch for his background. He is from my village in Ratnagiri and his uncle's mango orchard adjoins ours. He is very committed to learning. In fact, he even worked as a waiter in a hotel just to earn money to keep up his musical training.'

Ganpatrao didn't say a word. He stared at his left wrist and slowly turned it around. Dhondutai looked anxiously at him, waiting for a response. Ayi stood at the door, saying a silent prayer, hoping for a nod of approval. After a few minutes, Ganpatrao said, 'Let him come.'

A few days later, Sapre arrived at the door with a gaunt young man in a white kurta pajama.

'This is Sridhar Padhye,' said Sapre. Padhye greeted Ganpatrao and Ayi, touching their feet, and blurted with childlike pride, 'I have performed on stage.'

Dhondutai smiled kindly. Ganpatrao did not. Instead, he motioned for the young musician to sit behind the tabla set that lay in a corner of the room. It was examination time. He then proceeded to grill Padhye on esoteric rhythms and tempos, even ones that were not required in daily performance. Half an hour later, beads of sweat had formed across the young tabla player's temple, but he played on like an intrepid warrior. Dhondutai and Sapre watched the inquisition from two different corners in the room, knowing better than to interrupt or protest. Finally, Ganpatrao told Padhye he could leave. As he was leaving, he asked him his age.

'Twenty-five,' said Padhye.

'Married?'

'Just two months ago,' he replied, shyly.

'Hmmph,' was all Ganpatrao said, and opened the door.

Sapre looked a bit confused as he followed the mortified Padhye out. They both hurried down the stairs without looking behind. Ganpatrao stood at the top of the stairs, holding his elbows like an imperious headmaster watching his students scurry away.

The next morning, Padhye was woken up by a loud knock on his door. He looked sleepily at the table clock in the kitchen. It was just after six. The sky was beginning to light up and the birds had begun their morning ragas.

He opened the door and was jolted into full wakefulness when he saw his visitor. It was Ganpatrao, dressed formally in his coat, with cap and stick.

'Anna, you? Please… come in.' Padhye crossed his legs awkwardly to try and cover his bareness, for he was clad only in a pair of pajamas.

'No. It's quite alright. I am out for my morning walk and must carry on. I have to make it to the flower-sellers before the market gets too crowded. I just came to tell you that Dhondutai would like you to start from next week. You may come on Monday morning at ten.'

Padhye stared at him for a few seconds. Then he mumbled, 'Thank you.'

'By the way, I forgot to ask. Who is your teacher?'

'Yeshwant Kerkar,' said Padhye, happy to pronounce his revered guru's name so early in the morning.

'Wah,' said Ganpatrao. He patted the young musician on his shoulder, briskly turned around, and strode down the corridor. Padhye couldn't see Ganpatrao's expression, but the old curmudgeon was smiling to himself, thinking, 'Unbelievable!' Dhondutai's new accompanist was a student of Kesarbai's accompanist. It was a miraculous coincidence, where God winks and says, 'This one's for you, dear!' For, Kesarbai was insanely paranoid about people stealing her music. Even her accompanists—and, in turn, students' accompanists—were under suspicion and had to pass strict tests of loyalty before they had access to her. The fact that Padhye was her own tabla player's student would get him through with flying colors. One less reason to upset Mai, he thought to himself, with a smile and walked briskly down the street.

Padhye stared after Ganpatrao. He closed the door and latched it. He called out to his bride. 'You won't believe who just stopped by… ' And he chuckled to himself as he picked up his neem stick and wash mug and went to the little mirror that dangled on a thick wire next to the window.

Dhondutai once told me that it was because Padhye and she shared a legacy of gurus that she could relate to him so well musically and personally—that and the fact that he didn't drink! ('I know he smokes cigarettes, but as long as he doesn't do it in front of me, I am fine with that,' she said.)

There are so many nuances in the relationship between a musician and her accompanists. It's like the subterranean connection that develops between cousins. Due to sheer proximity, singer and accompanist develop a similar unspoken rapport over a period of time. They learn how to cover up for each other, how to preempt a mistake, and how to enhance each other's expression during performance.

One time, many years later after a combination of tobacco and age had caught up with him, Padhye was accompanying Dhondutai at a concert in Bombay in memory of Alladiya Khan. Before she started, she told her audience a little story. The old Khansahib used to be called 'Mr Difficult' because he had a penchant for singing complex and rare ragas. One day, a listener challenged him to sing something simple. He responded with his usual brilliance. He picked one of the simplest ragas, Desh, and a very basic taal, Rupak. But having done that, he sang a stunningly difficult composition, one that left the audience breathless.

That day, in his memory, Dhondutai sang the same piece. About ten minutes into it, when the piece was describing the visual beauty of Lord Krishna, Dhondutai suddenly stared at Padhye and opened her eyes wide at him in a gesture of disapproval. He smiled obliviously and continued playing. She motioned to me behind her to sing a stretch. While I took over from her, she hissed under her breath, 'Padhye. It's Rupak. What are you doing? You've slipped into Teentaal.' Padhye looked as if he had been caught with his zipper down at a crowded wedding. He realized what he had done and switched back to the beat that he was supposed to be playing. That was it. The ten second interaction between them went unnoticed by the thousand-odd people sitting in front, and what could have been a huge faux pas was seamlessly rectified.

There were many times when he covered for her as well. If she attempted a difficult movement and missed a beat when reaching the sama, he would muffle the last couple of beats by overplaying to distract the audience's attention. It was an unspoken code between them that would not be discussed other than in musical phrases, a relationship based on trust and mutual respect for human frailty.

Unlike many other tabla players, Padhye never pushed himself to the forefront. He was satisfied with his role as accompanist and teacher. Yet, every once in a while he would get a chance to display his rhythmic prowess and Dhondutai encouraged him wherever she could. Once, at a concert in Nagpur, in between two ragas, the audience requested a solo display of tabla. Padhye turned to Dhondutai and she nodded. He came into his own and regaled the audience with a ten minute show of different rhythmic patterns while she sat on stage and beamed at the response and applause. 'He is like my younger brother,' she often said. 'Why would I not support his growth?'

'Accompanists are like spouses,' Kesarbai once told Dhondutai. Even if they are not the best one to have, at some point habit takes over and you stick it out with each other. She was responding to Dhondutai's irritation over Abdul Majid Khan, Kesarbai's longtime sarangi accompanist. The two of them were known for conjuring up a magical chemistry on stage. The problem was, towards the end, he had grown quite hard of hearing and Dhondutai was forced to play the tanpura as close to his ear as possible. Frustrated with this unusual demand on her posture, she once said, 'Why don't you just get rid of him, mai? There are so many others out there who are as good.' Kesarbai didn't say anything. But at a performance the very next week, she asked another sarangi player to accompany her.

At the end of the show, as they wrapped the tanpuras in their covers, she turned to Dhondutai, 'So, how did you find him?'

'No, mai. Just not the same.'

'See. I told you so…'

Dhondutai realized that Majid Khan knew Kesarbai's music more intimately than anyone else in the world. Over the years, he had trained his bow to produce a broad, resonant sound, which truly seemed to replicate the voice of his beloved mai.

A few years into their lessons, Kesarbai told Dhondutai to go with her to Lonavla, a hill station a couple of hours away from Bombay. One of Kesarbai's wealthy friends had loaned them his bungalow. It was just the two of them and Kesarbai's granddaughter Ila, who was on vacation after her school exams. They sang undisturbed, day and night. They started with the early morning voice training that was so crucial to this gharana, stopping only for meals and a short afternoon nap. Ila was regularly bribed with ice cream so that she didn't disturb the lessons.

It was during these early morning practices that Dhon-dutai received what she had been anxiously waiting for—the voice culture training, which could transform even the most ordinary voice into one that worked wonders, with the perfect articulation of the 'aa', stamina, and breath control. They would start at five in the morning and sing into the dawn.

In their free moments, she listened to stories about how women like Kesarbai occupied that paradoxical space where they would entertain patrons until late into the night, and bathe and cover their forehead with ash in time for their four am ritual in front of the goddess.

Kesarbai also told her about how she used to love playing the stock market and the secret love she harboured for gambling. She tried to explain stocks and shares to Dhondutai, but it was like putting water in a sieve.

'You are a fool,' Kesarbai would say. 'Don't you have any interest in living well and wearing nice jewellery?'

'Ask me to learn how to make a taan swoop down like an eagle catching its prey, and I'll master it. But all this talk is completely uninteresting to me, mai.'

'You should develop different facets of your personality, girl. Sometimes, one part of you should not be able to tolerate the other. That's what makes a woman mysterious, unpredictable, even bizarre.'

'Mai. You and I are just too different,' Dhondutai would say with a laugh, trying to dodge the uncomfortable truths that were being thrown at her like darts which she gently deflected by strumming the tanpura and starting to sing.

Deep down, Dhondutai perhaps understood why her teacher was goading her, but she swiftly rearranged her thoughts and separated life from music. Being with Kesarbai had made her conscious of her almost abnormal chastity, but it was too late to do any thing about it. She didn't even have a choice in the matter, for what you become is sometimes beyond your control. They both had the same goal musically, but had been born to take different paths to achieve it. Dhondutai continued to treat music like celestial wisdom, not merely a profession.

Living together, the two women developed an understanding that gradually broke down the boundaries that marked their different worlds. All moral judgments were suspended. Dhondutai learned to understand why her teacher smoked one cigarette every morning to help her bowel movements. And Kesarbai cajoled her student into trying something she had never done before—eating eggs!

Kesarbai was an astonishingly good cook. Every time she traveled to a new place for a recital, she attempted to learn the specialties of that area. Over the years she had mastered numerous exotic dishes, including a delicious recipe known as the 'standing chicken' curry. This she had learned in Hyderabad, from the princes and nobles who ate it when they went out hunting. They would shoot the birds and cook them with whole onions, whole tomatoes and un-ground spices, in a giant pot, on an open fire in the jungle. There was no time to chop any of the ingredients and this, evidently, lent its own unique flavor to the dish. Her favorite was of course fish—which is what she ate every day from the time she was a child living in Goa. Right until the very end, she would make the time to grind her own spices for her special fish curry.

'Kesarbai tried to persuade me to try her chicken and meat dishes, suggesting that I needed the high protein diet to develop my musical stamina,' recalled Dhondutai, twisting her face and laughing. 'What was she thinking?' The young student didn't succumb to the pressure to eat meat, but she did start eating one egg every day—one of the few secrets she kept from her parents.

It was in Lonavla that Kesarbai loosened up and started to reveal the critical factors that transform a singer into a stage artiste. For, even though there were any number of stories about Kesarbai's derision towards her audiences, she was a committed professional. She would practice for days before a concert—which also explained why, in her heyday, she didn't have time to take on students.

'You have to make sure your audience receives the very best,' she told Dhondutai, recalling one of her concerts in Indore. 'I was to perform in the evening as well as the following morning, so that I could showcase different ragas. Before starting, I sang a ga in the lower octave and called out, "Can every one in the last row hear me?" A feeble voice from the back cried out, "No!" I promptly asked the program organizers to return the ticket money to those sitting in the last row and ensured that they had front row seats for the morning performance. That's how you have to treat your audience—they make or break an artiste.'

Back in Bombay, their lessons continued like clockwork, and Dhondutai didn't dare miss even one. The day she was too exhausted to do her early morning practice, Kesarbai immediately caught on and showered her with rebukes.

Being with Kesarbai was an entirely different experience from her earlier, more nurturing teachers, But after a few traumatic and bewildering episodes, Dhondutai figured out how to handle Kesarbai's temperament. If a particular taan was not going right or her stamina started waning, and she could sense Kesarbai beginning to lose patience, she quickly distracted her by saying something like, 'Mai, the other day I ran into so-and-so on the road and he was remembering the concert in which you sang Jaijaiwanti. He was full of praise for you mai...' The flattery usually did the trick. Kesarbai's tone changed and she melted.

'Yes, I do remember that concert. It was supremely good. Ha ha. That was the time when some cursed photographer tried to take pictures of me. I had to pull the film out of his camera because he didn't listen. God knows where these photos end up. If they go into a newspaper, it is the worst thing. The next thing you know, your face is being used to wipe some child's potty!'

'I agree mai. One has to be careful with these photo people. They may use the pictures to do black magic on you.'

By the time Kesarbai finished reminiscing, Dhondutai was able to regain her stamina, practice the piece in her head a couple of times, and restart with renewed vigor. By that point, Kesarbai would usually be her happy, self-absorbed self and less harsh with her student. It was quite a simple tactic. Dhondutai knew that she simply had to make her teacher feel like she was the queen of the universe. By toeing her line, you could win her trust and she would be willing to share her gems. If, on the other hand, anyone dared challenge her, or rub her the wrong way, 'she wouldn't even give them the dirt from her fingernails,' said Dhondutai, shaking her head and touching the tips of her earlobes in memory of her combustible teacher.

Little did Dhondutai realize, as she described her mildly scheming ways with Kesarbai, that I used to do exactly the same thing with her. In my case, it wasn't fear of eliciting her wrath, but boredom that drove me to try to distract Dhondutai from the lesson and propel her into meaningless conversation. The pattern was easy enough. I would start talking about a rival musician whose concert I had just attended and cough up an exaggerated report on how badly he sang, or how the auditorium was half empty. I knew how much she revelled in these verbal demolitions of her contemporaries. She would merrily add her own two-bit opinion. 'What do you expect? He knows two-and-a-half ragas and sings the same ones every time anyway.'

Her favorite moment was when I took off on a particular singer whom she considered her worst enemy. 'Baiji, guess what? I heard she arrived half an hour late to her own performance and then spent the next half an hour tuning her tanpura.' What she wouldn't hear from me, for it wouldn't suit my purpose, was that despite the singer's delay, the audience had waited patiently for her to begin and when she did, her music made up for every thing.

I tried, many times, to coax stories out of Dhondutai about her teacher's darker side, about the moments when she was the unwitting victim of this whimsical woman's outbursts. But she remained faithful to her guru, resorting instead to the deceptions of selective memory.

'There was only one time,' said Dhondutai with a laugh. 'I got so angry with her because of something she said, that I didn't go back to her house for days.'

'What happened?' I asked.

'Well, she said something rude about Laxmibai...'

Laxmibai Jadhav was one of the court singers of Baroda who later came to live in Kolhapur and taught Dhondutai for a couple of years after Bhurji Khan's death. Although it was a short period of training, both grew deeply fond of each other. Laxmibai was highly regarded in her time, but died young and remained relatively unrecognized as a result, for there were only a few recordings to carry her into the future.

'What did she say?' I asked, intrigued.

'She said that Laxmibai's taans were like the wagging movements of the woman laying cowdung on the floor.' In Marathi, the statement sounded startlingly crude.

After Kesarbai made this remark, Dhondutai did not go back the following Tuesday, or Friday, and didn't send word explaining her absence. Finally, Kesarbai sent someone to her house to ask what the matter was. After some convincing, Dhondutai went back to Parag.

Kesarbai was sitting on her bed scowling at her English tutor, Mary, when Dhondutai arrived. The elderly woman acted surprised and said, 'What happened to you? Where have you been?'

Dhondutai replied that she could not tolerate anyone saying anything nasty about her late guru. Kesarbai neatly defused the situation and said, 'My dear, I was only testing you to see your loyalty towards your teachers. Now I am convinced that even when I am not around, you will not tolerate anyone saying anything negative about me.' Dhondutai immediately forgave her and they went back to their lessons. However, Kesarbai was growing cantankerous and impatient. Age only exacerbated what was inherently her nature.

There are very few students who can emerge from the shadow of a great artist. They spend years echoing their notes, filling in gaps, and carrying instruments and flasks of tea to and from concerts. After a while, if they don't break away, most remain an echo of their master's voice.

I often tried to understand how a willful individual like Dhondutai stuck it out with a crazy witch like Kesarbai. Perhaps she was attracted to what she didn't have within her—the confidence to break all boundaries. Perhaps it was her innocence. Once she declared loyalty to anyone, she would stand by them no matter what.

'I heard that she didn't encourage you to perform on your own and prevented you from singing on the radio,' I continued to prod and probe.

'That's not true,' she retorted. 'In the beginning, yes, she didn't like me to give solo concerts, but that is because most teachers are wary of presenting their students to the public until they deem them fit representatives of their tutelage. Anyway, towards the end, especially after she was close to retiring, she sent me in her place to prestigious music festivals all over the country. So whoever said that is very mistaken.'

But I knew there had been terrible moments between them when Dhondutai had to suffer taunt after taunt in silence, just so that she could become a better musician. I could only imagine the scene, for there was no way of verifying what went on deep inside the house in Shivaji Park.

Could it be that Kesarbai had unfolded a raga, slowly undressing every note, singing it like she was making love to it, first in gentle caresses, then with all the vigour one reserves for a paramour, reaching a monumental climax with wave after wave of exhilaration? Could it be that when Dhondutai had attempted to sing it after her, she had been rebuked by her teacher and told that she would never be able to render passion because she had not experienced it?

I heard of one incident, when Kesarbai sat in front of her disciple and sang fifty short practice taans, then turned to her and said, 'Now repeat those.' She did it again and again, and grew increasingly angry because her student was not able to remember all of them. It was virtually impossible to memorize and then reproduce so many movements all at once.

Kesarbai's younger brother, Baburao, who happened to be sitting on the side, said, 'What are you doing? How can you expect her to follow that. Slow down, mai!'

'Stay out of this,' she had retorted sharply. 'She's a well-trained singer. She can pick them up.'

'Is this how Khansahib taught you?'

'What do you know?'

That evening, as Dhondutai was leaving, Baburao followed her out of the door and said, 'You'd better leave her. She is going to destroy you.'

One day, Dhondutai and Ganpatrao were sitting in Kesarbai's house, when an impresario showed up. He wanted to organize Kesarbai's concert in Pune.

'Ho! So you finally thought of coming to me,' said Kesarbai, with a snort. 'I notice that you have been hosting several concerts of that Malu. What brought you to me now? Did she lose her voice? Or did she stop sleeping with you? Hah! Well, anyway, I can't really make it, but you can have my student Dhondutai. Here, meet her. This is Dhondutai and this is her father Ganpatrao.'

Instead of approaching her father, which was the usual practice, the man went up to Dhondutai and shook her hand. His handshake lingered a moment too long and Dhondutai shrank back. She looked with terror at her father. Kesarbai started laughing. 'Don't be afraid. He won't bite, Dhondabai. You are not going to get very far if you behave like a coy bride all your life.'

Ganpatrao's expression turned steely and his moustache quivered. This was exactly the kind of thing he had dreaded. His daughter might be learning music, but she would not be treated like one of the bais. From the time she had started performing as a young girl, Ganpatrao had not allowed her to interact with anyone, whether it was a fan or an organizer. No one was permited to come up to her on stage right after a performance and tell her how much they enjoyed it. He stood there on constant guard, her public face. And now, this man was trying to get friendly with his daughter. She was not a 'Dhondabai' as her teacher had mocking described her.

He did not have the guts to say any thing to Kesarbai, but after a few minutes of uncomfortable silence, he mumbled something about it getting dark outside, and father and daughter left. They didn't speak much while on their way home, but later that evening, Ganpatrao said, 'Daughter, I don't know if I like the atmosphere in Bombay for a young woman singer. No matter what happens, I don't want you, in any way, to compromise your integrity. Just remember, that this is a divine art form, not some cheap performance racket. And even if you don't become rich or famous, you are singing for the goddess. That is all that counts. Treat your music with respect. Worship it. And always keep to yourself.'

His words may have been the cautionary words of a concerned father, but they had a resounding impact on Dhondutai's life. For, over the next couple of years, she became even more reclusive than before, cocooning herself in a space that had less and less to do with the world outside.

Creative people are often not able to handle failure.

They develop mechanisms to work around reality and tweak it to suit their own script. They also start living in a perpetual state of paranoia which sometimes drives them towards self destruction.

After the first few public concerts, Dhondutai began to feel the weight of her teacher's shadow on her. She was always compared to her, so that even if she sang reasonably well, it was never good enough. Dhondutai took every thing personally and started believing in the occult. At some point, she actually began to believe that Kesarbai was trying to pull her down. She suspected that her teacher couldn't bear the thought of anyone—even her own musical progeny—taking her place. She was not getting programmes, and was convinced that someone was deliberately jeopardizing her chances at success. The feelings grew more intense and every little thing played into her fears.

One day, while sitting at Parag, Dhondutai had an epiphany. One of the women of the house had brought three cups of tea, as was the custom. Dhondutai stared unhappily at the cup. The color was not right. What if someone had poisoned it? These women from Goa were known for their black magic. She pushed it away and said her stomach was not feeling too good.

'What's the matter with you today?' Kesarbai scowled at her. Dhondutai carried the cup back into the kitchen. She poured the tea into the sink and thought she heard a hissing sound as the liquid met the stone.

Bad omens come to people because they want them to. That evening, while getting off the bus, Ganpatrao tripped and fell. He grazed his knee and palm. As she helped her limping father up the slope that led to Anand Nagar,

Dhondutai thought to herself, 'I have nothing more to stay on for in Bombay. At the end of the day, my teacher is from a different world. Besides, I must look after my parents. They are also getting on in age.'

Her father seemed to echo her thoughts exactly and voiced his opinion over dinner that evening. 'I think we should go to Babu and Ratan in Delhi. They have been saying how difficult it is for them to cope with the children, with both of them working full time. I think the Bombay raga is reaching its end.' He laughed weakly at his own joke. Ayi silently thanked the goddess for she wanted, more than anything, to be with her son and grandchildren.

Dhondutai said it was a good idea. But deep inside her, she knew that she was running away. She was not able to keep pace with the city and the arbitrary nature of the performing world, even though these are precisely the periods that an artiste must stick out. The scene was changing too rapidly. Orthodox classicism was being over-taken by a new romanticism in music that was breaking the boundaries of the traditional gharana. Vocal music was being sidelined by instruments like the sitar, sarod, and santoor, which the younger audiences found easier to appreciate.

Performing artistes have to learn to be simultaneously thick-skinned and sensitive—they must layer themselves to cope with the hurt that sometimes comes with baring your soul in public, and yet remain true to their art.

Dhondutai had the best training anyone could ask for, and had the makings of a great performing artiste, but she did not attempt to understand the ways of the world and let go of her inhibitions. She did not realize that sometimes, a parent's protective instinct may be a reflection of his own fears. It can stunt and even kill the object of its love. It is possible that, if pushed, Dhondutai could have become a famous singer.

But this was not to be. On a hot October day in 1971, a week before Diwali, Dhondutai and her parents left Bombay.

As the train clanked its way across the country, Dhondutai was beset with a flurry of images and emotions. She remembered the time when she had accompanied Kesarbai on stage and her teacher suddenly sung a note which was not supposed to feature in that particular raga. Dhondutai was shocked. What was she doing? Then her teacher turned around and pinched her, the way she used to when she wanted to share a joke, smiled, and whispered. 'Look at the fools! They love what I'm singing. They're too stupid to tell the difference.' She remembered how Kesarbai was once outraged to see the first couple of rows of a concert hall lying empty. They had been reserved for sponsors, who had not shown up. The real music lovers were in the cheaper balcony seats. Although she was a stickler for starting on time, she refused to begin until the organizers agreed to let the balcony crowd come down and occupy the empty seats. When they protested, she said, 'Why don't I place hundred rupee notes on these seats and sing for them!' Dhondutai fell asleep to the rocking motion of the train and dreamt about a morning in Lonavla. Raga Bhairavi. Dark mint tea. And the sun rising from behind a hill.

A biographer writing about Dhondutai years later may suggest something along these lines. Just when Dhondutai was coming into her own as an artiste, in her early forties, she decided to move to Delhi for reasons that are inexplicable. She had no support there. Her family had no connections in the music world and were somewhat isolated, living in the suburb of Ghaziabad. In Bombay, she had access to the best musicians and connoisseurs, who would have done anything for her because she carried the mantle of one of the greatest singers alive. In some ways, it was Dhondutai herself who sabotaged her career.

Seven

An old woman lay curled up on a bed, her sari loosely wrapped around her. She stared out of the window at the tree with fragrant white flowers. Passersby now regularly stole the buds, breaking entire branches in the process. Kesarbai grit her teeth when she thought about it. She raised her arm slightly as if to protest, then let it drop over the side of her bed. On a shelf, which hadn't been dusted for days, lay an array of trophies, including the silver veena which had been presented to her when she earned the title 'Surshri' after a path-breaking concert in Calcutta.

Outside, the hall which had once resounded with music and revelry was now silent. The instruments had been given away. The tabla set had gone to Yeshwant Kerkar, the sarangi had gone to its longtime player, Majid Khan. The tanpura stayed, but later went to Shantibhai's old friend, Manjutai, who lived a few houses down the road in Shivaji Park. It was better that way. She could not bear to see them lying there, untouched, wracking reminders of where she had once been. Kesarbai was seventy-four when she found that she was unable to deliver her best to her audiences. Unlike most other musicians who dragged themselves on stage even after their voices quivered with age and their stamina gave way, Kesarbai was one of the few who took voluntary retirement. One day, after a concert where her voice failed her and her famous taans fell flaccid, she decided to stop singing in public. She wanted to be remembered as a great singer. Soon after this, her body gradually deteriorated and she was afflicted with one illness after another. For the first time in her life, she gave up the fight. Music was over; she no longer had anything to fight for.

The family drifted in and out of the room, tiptoeing lest they woke her and unleash another bout of anger and pain. They were more frightened by the sight of this frail woman wilting away into oblivion than they were by her usual tempestuous self.

'Mai, can we do anything for you?' Sumantai whispered, gently straightening her mother's hair the way one would a child's.

'Make me some sol curry and fried fish,' replied Kesarbai in a hoarse whisper.

Sumantai went back down to her apartment and started grinding the spices to make her mother's favorite foods, knowing well that her tastebuds would scarcely recognize the flavors. She bore no grudges against her mother, even though many years ago, when she decided to get married and go away, Kesarbai had virtually broken ties with her and chosen to live with her sister's son on the floor above. She was angry that her daughter was leaving her to live her own life. For many years after, she refused to speak to her. It was one of the many ironies in Kesarbai's life: a woman who had been subjected to male chauvinism throughout, had eventually opted to live with her nephew and not her daughter—because she was the girl who went away, and he bore the family name and stayed in Parag.

Her grandchildren, nieces, nephews, all milled around her, trying to entertain her. But every invalid knows that even loved ones get exhausted with caretaking. Besides, there were already strains among family members. It was hardly surprising; Kesarbai was leaving behind a formidable inheritance.

Long before Kesarbai fell ill, Sumantai and her husband came to live on the floor below her, but they were not allowed up. When Dhondutai walked down the stairs after her lessons, Sumantai often stood at the door and whispered, 'How is she? Everything well?' She knew better than to take things personally with her mother. Even though Kesarbai rejected her affection, she cared deeply about her until the end.

Over the years, Kesarbai broke ties with all her well-wishers. One by one, they stopped coming to see her. She revelled in her loneliness. The diva who had once commanded the world couldn't bear to see herself as a pathetic dependent.

'Your old friends keep calling, mai,' said Suman softly, straightening the sheets on her bed. 'They want to see you.'

'I don't wish to see any goddamn person. Tell them I have died.' She turned around and faced the wall.

One of the few times she agreed to meet anyone was when an old friend, a well-known stage singer, Jyotsana Bhole, came to visit with some friends. She was feeling better that day and agreed to meet them. They came upstairs and sat with her, chatting about old times. Then Kesarbai said, 'Jyotsana, I am very keen to hear an old song by you. Please sing it for me.'

Her request was for a popular song which had evoked great emotion when it first came out. It was about an elderly person crying that the people whom she had once invited to her home had now taken it over and wanted her out. It had a double meaning. It was also how India felt about the British. Jyotsna Bhole sang it with tears in her eyes. Before leaving, she hugged the ailing artiste. No one asked Kesarbai why she remembered that song in particular.

Just before Kesarbai died, Dhondutai was in Bombay for a concert and came to Parag to see her teacher. She was appalled at the apparition that lay before her. A woman who once wore only the best chiffons and silks, was covered in a thin cotton sari. It fell loosely around her emaciated body. She didn't want to touch her food. The room was bare except for a locked cupboard which still contained some valuables. Dhondutai noticed the family huddled at the door.

'I think they were trying to see if mai was complaining to me about something,' said Dhondutai, her eyes brimming over, when she recounted that day for me. 'They didn't even bother clipping her nails or changing her sheets regularly.'

Kesarbai called out to her nephew and said, 'Tell Sonu to prepare a special meal. Today Dhondabai and I will eat together at the table.' Dhondutai looked away from her teacher with an expression of pain. They hadn't told Kesarbai that her beloved sister Sonu had died a few months ago. A few minutes later, Kesarbai forgot what she had just asked for and suddenly turned to Dhondutai. 'Sing Bihagda for me.' Dhondutai picked up the tanpura, ran the end of her sari across its stem in an attempt to wipe off the dust of months of neglect, and started singing the same raga that she had sung when she first met Kesarbai almost twenty years ago, one heady evening at Birla Matoshri Hall. Before she started the second alaap, she noticed that Kesarbai had fallen asleep, her mouth slightly open. Dhondutai couldn't bear to stay long. She touched her teacher's feet for the last time and ran out of the house.

Kesarbai died a year later, on the day the city celebrated the homecoming of Ganesha. It was a rainy day in September 1977. Somewhere circulating many miles above the Earth's surface, was a haunting song rendered by her. The words were 'Jaat kahaan hoe.' Where are you going...

Eight

It was a cold winter in Delhi, mitigated only by the afternoon sun that licked the floor tiles and created a mirage of warmth. Babu and his wife Ratan were both at work and the children were at school. Dhondutai bustled around the kitchen, making tea for the visitor who had come to see her father. Ganpatrao sat outside with the visitor. He spoke slowly, with some effort. He was almost ninety.

After drinking tea, Ganpatrao said he was feeling tired and excused himself. He went into his room, lay down next to his sleeping wife and died.

When Dhondutai came inside to check on her father, and press his feet as she often did when he lay down, she instantly knew. Praying silently, she went outside and phoned first her brother, and then the family physician.

When the doctor arrived, Ayi was stirring. She sat up slowly on the bed and saw the still body of her husband lying next to her. She slowly eased back onto the bed and shut her eyes, her lips quivering. Her body convulsed ever so slightly. The doctor rushed to her side and lifted her wrist. Her pulse had dropped to an alarming level. He quickly motioned to Dhondutai to rub her mother's feet to get her blood circulation going.

He had seen this once before. When a life partner dies, the one left behind can experience a near-death sensation.

It didn't surprise him. He knew that Ganpatrao and Sonatai's lives had been so closely intertwined for so many years that when one shut his eyes the other fell asleep; when one grazed her elbow, the other felt the pang of pain.

Ayi was revived and the family calmly went about the rituals for him. Dhondutai did not let her pain show. That is the way he would have wanted it.

Some months later, Dhondutai received this letter from Kesarbai's old friend Shantibhai:

December 1, 1978

Dear Dhondutai,

I heard about the passing on of Ganpatrao and offer you my deepest condolences. He was a man of great conviction. Every artist needs a muse to help them achieve their goals. He was that person for you. The way in which he broke all social barriers to get you into music is remarkable. He was clearly the constant presence in your life and I am sure you will miss him terribly. May God give you and Ayi the strength to withstand his loss. My respects also to your brother and his family.

As you know, we sorely miss the presence of Kesarbai in our lives and now must do something to keep her memory alive. I urge you to consider coming to Bombay. We will do whatever we can to help you get programmes as well as a few teaching assignments. I have already spoken to a friend and there are a couple of people who would be interested in learning from you, including my friend Manjutai, whom you have already met. We will also help you find lodgings. If you decide to bring Ayi, that would be even better. I am sure she would like to be with you. Just remember, we are all with you.

We have now set up a scholarship in mai's name. Any student who qualifies will get a small sum towards their teaching every month. We hope that this will keep her name alive and allow many others to pursue this art with the same unconditional passion that she did.

Our best regards to your brother and his family. Once again, please accept our sincere condolences.

Yours,
Shantibhai

A few months later, Dhondutai moved to Bombay with Ayi and five thousand rupees. Shantibhai and his friends had looked around for accommodation which would be appropriate for two single women. They learned of a widow who was a trained nurse and had a flat which she was interested in sharing with another woman. It was the perfect fit. She would look after Ayi whenever Dhondutai traveled for concerts. They agreed on a rent of four hundred rupees per month.

This was how Dhondutai met Mausi and moved into a small flat with pale green walls, opposite a brothel under Kennedy Bridge.

Part V
Kolhapur

One

The train pulled into the station at five-fifty in the morning, a few minutes before time. The attendant ambled past our seats, picking up the debris of crumpled sheets, and announced indifferently that we had arrived in Kolhapur.

'Where else would we be? Kolkata? Hee hee.' Dhondutai muttered under her breath, laughing. She turned to me. 'Come on, gather your things.' She adjusted her sari, patted her hair into place, and put her slippers on meticulously, first left, then right. We were the last ones to get off the train. I helped her off the steps, holding her purse until her feet touched the platform, and then jumped out, expecting to see the usual filth and frenzy that comes with Indian train stations. Instead, I was overwhelmed by the salubrious air of a small town and saw an empty platform that stretched out languidly. In a far corner, an old man sat on a bench listening to an abhang on his radio. As we walked by him, Dhondutai stopped to place a one rupee coin next to him.

She said, 'When you have crossed seventy-five years, it is time to start giving back. You can't take everything with you when you go. And we are all now in queue at Yama's door, so our time could come any time.'

I gave her a quick hug, thankful for twenty-five years of her wisdom. We looked around us. The station looked like a set from a period film. The main building was a quaint, neo-gothic structure with a short tower ending in an iron weather vane that swung gently against a cobalt sky. It had been named Chhatrapati Shahu Maharaj Station after the good prince who had once transformed this princely state into a musical haven.

A week earlier, I had been sitting before my teacher in her Borivli apartment, trying to learn Raga Jaijaiwanti. It is a soulful raga, built on the stunning juxtaposition of two gas, one flat, the other sharp. It happened to be one of Kesarbai's signature ragas, one she performed regularly. Unfortunately, her best recording of the raga, in which Dhondutai had given substantial back up, lay in a dusty archive in a musical academy in Calcutta.

The verse described a woman fretting because her husband had a lover. 'Who can I turn to and talk about my torn heart…?' It had been written by 'Sajeele,' a name which featured in numerous compositions I had heard and sung.

'Who is Sajeele?' I asked.

'That is the pen name of Alladiya Khan's maternal grandfather, who also taught him. He was an exponent of the Gauhar bani, a dhrupad style. In fact, one of the secrets of Alladiya Khan's gharana is that it is an amalgamation of three powerful styles. Khansahib's grandfather Sajeele sang the Gauhar bani, his father sang the Dagar bani, and his uncle Jahangir Khan sang the Khandhar bani.'

Clearly, Alladiya Khan's parents had been joined in marriage with the strategic intent of bringing together three musical tributaries. The human offspring was merely an aside, the real fruit of this union being the emergence of a new musical style.

I tried to picture an ancient bearded man who liked to call himself Sajeele, sitting on an old brocade sofa teaching the young grandson seated at his feet, in between deep drags on a sheesh pipe.

But my voice was not catching the notes. I sounded tired and hoarse. I tried again, but it just wasn't flowing. I always seemed to hit a note just a hairline short of the right pitch, making my teacher cringe. I looked at her desperately.

'You haven't slept well, have you?' she said, softly. 'What is the matter with you? You have been distracted for the last couple of days? You cannot go on like this. It's a waste of your time and mine...' The singing voice is the ultimate barometer of a person's mental and physical health. It hides nothing.

'I have some issues at home...' I faltered. I then unburdened myself, all the while strumming the tanpura softly as I spoke. I was thirty-six, entering the tenth year of my marriage, and with a baby boy. She didn't probe too much and let me leave out the details, but understood the sentiment: I felt like my life was falling apart.

'This is why I never got married. You cannot have two masters. It has to be music or a man. Both demand too much from one. I've seen my sister and so many others. There is no end to family issues. If it's not one thing, it's another. Husband. In-laws. Children. Sickness... Thankfully, I have been only answerable to myself—and to my music.'

Her voice softened. 'I know you don't believe in such things, but trust me, if you listen to what I tell you, things will get better. Let's go and visit the Mahalaxmi temple in Kolhapur. There, you must pray with all sincerity, and I will do the same for you. Believe me, if you approach the goddess, she takes care of you. But remember, when things work out, you must go back to thank her. I also need to go and thank her for sending me the answer to what has been bothering me for so many days. I didn't tell you what happened, did I?'

A few months ago, Dhondutai had woken up with a start in the middle of the night. The tap in the bathroom had not been twisted tightly shut so, every five seconds, a drop of water fell into the steel bucket with a loud, musical splosh. She sat up and looked at the round clock with fluorescent numerals on its face. It was four in the morning. The heat was unbearable and the fan was circulating thick, warm air. She decided to get herself a drink of water.

A moon beam had lit up the kitchen counter so she didn't have to switch on the light. Dhondutai reached for the steel tumbler and poured herself a glass. She thought of the letter from her brother which had arrived that afternoon. He told her that it was time for her to come and live with him in Delhi. She was old, almost eighty. Her health was deteriorating and it was not right for her to be alone any more. She thought about it. Yes, she felt vulnerable. If she were to fall and break a bone, who would be there to help her, to bathe her? She remembered the time she had managed to fight off two burglars when she was living in Ghaziabad many years ago and felt a wave of invincibility come over her. And what about her students? Would she have anyone to talk music with in Delhi? Would her brother's grandchildren resent having her around? Would she resent having all of them around? The thoughts raced through her faster than a Jaipur taan and she felt herself reeling. She clutched the granite platform and braced herself.

Over the next couple of weeks, without telling anyone, she listlessly started the process of shutting down her Bombay operations. She reluctantly walked into the real estate agent's office down the road and gave him details about her flat. 'Remember, it has the greatest vibrations any one could ask for,' she said, a tad sharply to the agent, who professed complete agreement with a practiced, 'Of course, madam!'

Her greatest concern was her little gods and goddesses. Should she be packing them up and taking them with her, or should she immerse them in the ocean. At this age, anything could happen to her, and then the gods would be left uncared for, unkempt. She shuddered at the thought. They had been with her more than sixty years, and had traveled everywhere with her all the way from Kolhapur to Delhi to Bombay. But there was no one after her. She couldn't rely on her family members, who might or might not share her faith. She had better set them free in the Arabian Sea. Her heart sank at the finality of it all.

The real estate agents started dropping in, bringing customers who would breeze in and out indifferently, intrusively. She was professional about it, and did not mind them peering into her rooms, looking questioningly at her instruments, and asking her questions about the water supply.

Then, one morning, she woke up as usual when the rooster announced the break of day. She sat down for her early morning practice, and started Raga Bhairavi. As she hit the higher notes, she saw a light enter the room. She had a vision of the goddess, and heard her sigh with pleasure.

It was a message. It all came together. She knew she had to stay for the sake of her music. Her goddess was telling her that she would protect her, and that she must proceed on her mission. It was not yet time to retire.

People who live on their own often 'see' visions or hear voices. Thus, the apparition may or may not have been a manifestation of Dhondutai's subconscious mind, telling her to be true to herself.

She looked at me. 'I need to thank the goddess for the answer and you need to ask your questions,' she said. 'We must go to Kolhapur.'

Even if I was cynical about bribing gods with promises of penance I loved the idea of visiting my teacher's muse. The goddess had nurtured and protected the greatest musicians. I would go and sing to her. She would hear my half-faith in my half-notes.

'Baiji, I'd really like to sing at the temple. Teach me something appropriate.'

Dhondutai smiled. 'I don't know the protocol of whether we can sing there any more. But here, learn this.' She taught me a song I had heard on Kesarbai's 78 rpm. It was a tribute to the goddess, in Raga Sukhiya Bilawal: 'Devi, the protector of good people and the slayer of evil...'

That very evening, Dhondutai pulled out her lunar calendar. The front listed important days. At the back, in fine pink print, was a detailed schedule of every train that crisscrossed India. This calendar was an essential in every traditional Maharashtrian home. One side featured critical information about journeys to be taken, the other side warned of travel dates that should be avoided because of moon phases and star alignments. We should go on Tuesday or Wednesday next week, Thursday is not a good day for journeys, she murmured to herself.

The next day, we both walked through a downpour to get to a travel agency down the road from her house to buy our Kolhapur train tickets. After scrutinizing the train and moon schedules, Dhondutai had decided that the Mahalaxmi Express would be most suitable. It left late in the evening and arrived early in the morning.

At the travel agency, a cheeky girl in a low cut, sleeveless shirt tried to explain to Dhondutai that even if she couldn't get her a lower berth, the conductor would 'adjust' with someone. The girl winked at me.

'My dear girl, don't think me to be a fool. I am a classical musician. I have traveled all over the country for concerts since the time I was ten years old. I want a confirmed lower berth,' said Dhondutai in a mock-stern voice.

'Oh wow! A singer! I want to learn music. Especially old film songs.'

The girl winked at me again. Luckily, Dhondutai didn't see her. I looked away and watched a man with buck teeth shout dates into the phone. The girl told us they would deliver the tickets the next day and handed over the receipt, which said 'Bone Voyage'.

As we parted ways on the curbside, Dhondutai turned to me and said, above the din of main road traffic, 'Go home carefully, dear.' She stepped back to avoid being splashed with foul black water as a rickshaw angrily scuttled past her. I should have uttered those words to her instead of the other way around, I thought, ashamed of my indifference, or laziness, or self-consciousness, or whatever it was that prevented me from hugging her and saying, 'I am so grateful for your presence in my life, baiji.'

On the way back home, all I could think of was the short, hunched figure waiting to cross the road while the traffic callously whizzed past. How alone she looked in a world that had grown too impatient for the solitary echoes of a five-foot-nothing singer.

As soon as the tickets were delivered, Dhondutai called Baba and informed him that we were coming to see him. When I went there the next day, she said, 'I woke up hiccupping this morning. I'm sure Baba is thinking of me and looking forward to seeing us. It has been more than ten years since we met.'

She then admonished me light-heartedly. 'Why did you have to state my real age on the ticket? You know I don't look any where near seventy-seven. I hardly have any grey hair. The conductor might question whether I am really the person on the ticket.' I smiled and said that we would tell him she dyed her hair to stay young.

Dhondutai was palpably excited about returning to her birthplace. The last time she had been back was at least fifteen years ago, for a concert. This was the town that had cajoled the notes out of her, where she had found mentorship with the greatest voices of the time, where she had given her first radio performance at the age of eight and been dubbed a child star, where she had been propositioned with roles in the early black-and-white 'talkies.'

'Let's plan our three days properly so that we can achieve all the things we have set out to do.'

'Good idea, baiji. You decide the itinerary. I am in your hands.'

'We arrive in the morning, right? We will first freshen up. You will get some authentic Maharashtrian breakfast of puffed rice and tea,' she chuckled. 'Then we will head to the temple. If I remember right, the morning prayers are at eight-thirty. We must make it in time. Then we can just walk around the temple precinct and I'll show you the old palace and the small private Bhavani temple where Alladiya Khan used to sing for the king. After lunch, we can rest for a while. Then we will all go to Baba's place… '

'And your house. I want to see the place where you grew up!'

'Yes, of course, whatever is left of it. They've cut down all the trees… But we can go there. Maybe that old family that used to live across the road is still there. I remember there was a foolish singer who would come and stay with them just so that he could eavesdrop on the Khansahib's lessons with me,' she said, with a giggle.

I shared her excitement. I was intrigued to meet Baba again after at least fifteen years. Did he still wear the same sharkskin safari suits? Would he twinkle at me from behind his opaque glasses? And the Mahalaxmi temple had always been a source of wonder for me.

'What should I take for him? Maybe a shawl and a nice grey suit-piece?'

'Money is best,' replied Dhondutai.

On Tuesday evening, the day of Ganesha, Dhondutai and I boarded the train at Dadar. The long-distance trains shared a platform with the local trains, something we weren't quite prepared for. It was the height of rush hour. While we were walking down the ramp to get to platform four, I heard a local train approaching. Suddenly, a tidal wave of men and women mobilized out of nowhere and dashed maniacally down the ramp. They would have drowned out the little figure next to me, had I not pushed her against the railing and protected her from the onslaught. Dhondutai was no longer in a position to take on the self-absorbed agitation of Bombay. She was best off in her protective cocoon with her tanpuras standing guard.

The train arrived on time, finding its place on the platform half a minute before and just after a local train, in that miraculous way that Bombay's transport system achieves its precarious balance in the midst of unimaginable chaos. Once we had made it safely on board, we were at ease. Two men sat on the berth across from us. Dhondutai was quick to point out that they were occupying our seat, but one of them gruffly informed her that they were railway employees and would get off at the next stop.

I got Dhondutai two pillows from the train attendant so that she could sit back comfortably. Soon we both settled down to the rhythm of the tracks. Train journeys have a wonderful way of turning into story telling sessions, latent memories and forgotten anecdotes coming to the fore, especially when travelling companions are complete strangers.

'So tell me a little about Kolhapur,' I said.

'Well, it was called 'Kalapur' because of the number of great artists and artisans it attracted. What is it not known for? Painting, jewellery—haven't you seen typical Kolhapuri jewellery?—crafts, film production, sports, especially wrestling and of course, music and dance.'

'Well, these days, it is better known as the sugar capital and a place where leather slippers are crafted,' I said.

'Yes, times have certainly changed. The later kings were not aesthetes like Shahu Maharaj. They were more interested in horse racing. But someone or the other has continued to sponsor music, sometimes quite unexpectedly—like the man who managed the Kolhapur Sugar Mills. His name was Madan Mohan Lohia. Despite being a Marwari businessman, he was a die hard music lover and did whatever he could to help music. He would give jobs to unemployed musicians in his factory store, even the ones who could barely read and write. If they had a concert, or an important lesson, he would tell them to clock in and then go and practice undisturbed. Why! Even Baba worked as a storekeeper at the Kolhapur Sugar Mills for more than thirty years, after he discovered that he couldn't really make it as a musician.'

Dhondutai then described an all-night concert sponsored by the sugar mill at the Panhala fort on the outskirts of the city. It was a uniquely choreographed evening: Dhondutai and the ghazal and thumri queen Begum Akhtar had been asked to perform all night long, alternately, for hour-long sessions.

I thought I saw a flicker of interest in one of the men who sat across from us. The other one continued to read his newspaper.

Dhondutai shook her head and touched her ear. 'What a woman! She was a chain smoker. On stage, she had a cigarette in one hand and played the harmonium with the other. It was a sight to behold. With her twinkling nose-ring and her seductive voice...'

'How old were you, baiji?'

'Oh, I must have been around twenty. Akhtaribai was much older... already a name to reckon with. I sang classical music, she sang lighter forms.'

'What a beautiful concept, to have you performing in alternating, undulating sessions all night!'

'Yes. It really was fun, though I was a bit concerned about the smoke getting into my throat. To start with, my father wasn't pleased about me singing at such an event, after all I was girl from a good family. But Baba convinced him that it was in my best interest.'

I could see that the man across from us was now listening keenly to our conversation. He looked up from his book, which he had evidently not been reading, and said, 'My grandfather used to live on the same street as Akhtaribai in Lucknow. As a child, I have heard her singing.' He spoke with a north Indian accent, which seemed as if it had grown stronger because it was emboldened by nostalgia.

'Grandfather used to tell me the story of how this barrister had agreed to marry her on the condition that she stop singing, except for him. That was the price she had to pay for respectability. For more than ten years, no one heard her voice. Then, she fell terribly sick with an illness that the best doctors were not able to diagnose. Finally, one doctor, suggested that she was suffering from depression, and that the only cure for her was to sing again.'

'So the world got Begum Akhtar back,' murmured Dhondutai.

'So much for the barrister...' I said.

Dhondutai smiled and turned to the stranger. 'So, are you fond of music?'

'Well, I don't claim to be a connoisseur, but growing up in Lucknow, I listened to a lot of semiclassical music. Now, living in Bombay, working as an engineer with the railways, and commuting three hours a day, I only listen to the sound of the tracks. But I think I am going to start carrying a little portable player with me... Meeting you has inspired me!'

He folded his hands respectfully and got up to leave. His stop was drawing near. Before he left, Dhondutai reached into her bag and pulled out a cassette. It was a self-published compilation of select pieces from her concert recordings.

'Here. Why don't you take this to start with, a present from me.'

The man was visibly moved. He touched her feet and took off, clutching the small gift that would help him soar again, even while sitting on a rexine train seat.

Dhondutai was pleased with herself. After the strangers had left, she put her feet up on the seat opposite her and dozed off for a little while. I read.

The attendant had started distributing the sheets and blankets for the night when Dhondutai woke up. She was smiling. 'You won't believe this! I dreamt about the Nandi bull next to the lake where we used to go for a walk as children. It's a giant stone statue. They say it moves to the extent of two grains of wheat forward, and the length of one sesame seed backwards, every year.'

'Sort of like my musical training,' I said with a laugh.

'Yes. And the story goes that when the bull finally falls into the lake, the world will come to an end.'

'Oops. We'd better go there and check how far it is from the water, and then prepare for the worst,' I said, laughing.

'Don't smirk like that. You know, at the rate things are going, the world will definitely be coming to an end. Luckily, I won't be around to see that.'

The scent of fresh parathas soaked in ghee wafted in from the cabin next door. Passengers were opening their packed dinners and food was being passed around amongst fellow travellers. Dhondutai had painstakingly prepared a meal of stuffed parathas and curd rice and she lay it on the berth, alongside my more meager offering of vegetables and yoghurt.

'Wait till you try what I have made. You'll see how, whether it is singing or cooking, I do the best!'

After dinner, I helped Dhondutai to the toilet. While she was washing up, I made our beds and tried to ignore a baby mouse that scurried past my slipper, probably seeking a tidbit from the delicious meal prepared by my music teacher.

Like most small towns in India, Kolhapur has a truncated downtown built around the statue of a local hero—the warrior king Shivaji. Addresses and directions are usually given in relation to the three important landmarks of the city—the Mahalaxmi temple, the Shivaji statue, and the old palace. So, Mr so-and-so lives in the temple lane, or the farmer's market is opposite the old palace.

As we entered the town centre, I could see remnants of a glorious history emanating from behind shop facades and buildings. These ruins were trying to find contemporary relevance. A magnificently carved facade dotted with gargoyles had become the front for a women's underwear store; the space beneath the two stone elephants guarding the temple was being used for shelter by a flower vendor, who hung his garlands on their chipped tusks. The most disengaged from their past were the old palace buildings which had been taken over by various government offices, guaranteeing their speedy fall into ruin.

We entered the massive portals that led to the temple complex. Like a mini township, it was filled with smaller temples, shops, offices, homes, and of course thousands of people milling in and out, seeking solace, begging forgiveness, offering gratitude. The main Mahalaxmi temple was at the centre of it all, a monument towering above the chaos.

'See these guards?' said Dhondutai, like a proud tour guide, pointing at two statues standing erect on either side of the gate. 'They built this temple overnight and then froze here.' She strode in like someone returning to their parental home, staking their claim on a past life. A couple of flower vendors came up to her. She bought the lotuses that were the goddess' favorite flower, after arguing with the seller that his buds were wilting. Further down, she picked up a sari for the goddess—which would no doubt find its way right back to the shop by the end of the week, via a well-oiled line of corrupt priests.

Devotees flocked towards the temple, bending to touch the stone steps as they entered. Some of them had walked barefoot from their villages many miles away. The morning prayers were beginning. Soon, we became part of a murmuring stream of humanity with its own force chanting its way towards the altar, stopping only to place an offering before the goddess and collect a holy 'return present' which was clutched in sweaty palms, to be distributed to eager relatives waiting at home.

I stared at the goddess, who had been abandoned by her consort and found a beautiful place of her own here on the banks of the Panchganga river. I believe in you, I thought, but I cannot bring myself to focus in a place like this. My worship needs solitude.

'Wait...' hissed Dhondutai.

She'd seen something. I stopped and peered in the direction she was looking. In the shadows, I could see an alcove a few feet away, where there was a small shrine. All I saw was the usual vermillion streaks on a vague amorphous stone god, and a scattering of flowers and coins in front of it. It was Ganesha. What had caught her attention?

'I saw a mouse,' whispered Dhondutai. 'Ganesha's mouse has run off. It is the most auspicious sign, my dear. Ganesha is pleased you are here. You are very lucky. Let's go now. We'll come back early tomorrow morning and sing.'

As we were walking out, through the maze of columns, she stopped before one and caressed it. This was the place where Alladiya Khan had sat and sung in his time, leaning against this pillar. For a long time, there was a stain on it from the oil in his hair, she pointed out. I peered at the column and thought I saw the smudge.

We came out of the temple complex and walked around the precinct, towards the old palace and a smaller Bhavani temple which was used privately by the king and his select courtiers. It was a gorgeous square courtyard, under a translucent roof which let in natural light. A first-floor gallery above ran along all four sides. This was where the queens and their ladies would sit and listen to musicians and watch dancers and performers. A mammoth chandelier hung from the ceiling, swinging ever so gently, perhaps so as not to disturb the delicate cobwebs that appeared and disappeared in the late morning light.

'I heard Alladiya Khan sing here during the Navratri festival,' said Dhondutai. 'It was a grand seven-day affair, when the biggest names from all over the country came and performed. The queen was very fond of me and invited me and my sister to attend.'

Perhaps it was the filtered lighting, or the serene, abandoned air of the place, but it had become like a sanctuary for people looking for a brief respite from the outside world. People strolled in and sat around, opening their tiffin boxes for their mid-morning snack, or even laying down for a quick nap.

We walked out into the harsh light. 'What should we do now?' I asked. 'Let's walk around some more? I know what! Let's go see the house where you used to live.'

Dhondutai was a little tired, so we decided to take a rickshaw. We bumped our way through a crisscross of small lanes and came to the garden. 'Now just make a left here...' The rickshaw stopped at a nondescript two-storey stone building. A young woman sat on a stool at the front door. She was sifting through a tray of wheat kernels, separating the chaff from the grain. Two children played in front of her. I stared at the building, trying to conjure up the sight of a young Ayi sitting in the same spot. We asked the rickshaw to wait for a minute.

'They've built it up completely,' said Dhondutai a little angrily. 'This is not the building. Where we used to live is behind this, you can't even see it. This used to be where the garden was, which we would let out for marriage functions. I don't know why we've bothered to come here at all.'

The children stopped playing and ran to their mother, conscious of strangers intruding on their space.

'This lady used to live here... sixty years ago,' I said with a smile, to the woman sitting there. She stared at us blankly.

I could tell Dhondutai didn't wish to hang around. We got back into the rickshaw and she said we should go and see the lake down the road, where her father would take the three children for a walk at half past five every morning.

'We hated him for forcing us to get up at the crack of dawn and do this long walk, but it is his discipline that has kept me in such good health today,' said Dhondutai with a laugh. A flock of herons fluttered by. The rickshaw stopped. I gasped. We were standing in front of a gorgeous lake. A cobbled pathway and a wrought iron railing ran around its three-and-a-half mile circumference.

Dhondutai beamed with pride. 'Isn't it beautiful?'

'And that too, right in the heart of the city!' I said.

'Come, let's walk some of the way. I'll show you the well into which I and my brother would stop to throw stones and wait for the distant "plop."' She seemed to have revived, and the cool stillness of the water, the cackle of geese and the laughter of women washing clothes, put her back on track.

'My father walked the full round of the lake. We had to keep up with him, so we would end up running while he strode briskly. We would return just after the man with the buffalo had been around; three tall glasses of freshly-squeezed milk would be waiting for us. In those days, no one had heard of boiling or pasteurizing milk. You drank it straight up.'

A white-headed eagle swooped around, circling the lake. We passed by a bed of flowers. Dhondutai bent to pick up an orange and red blossom. 'See this. The famous Kolhapur earrings were designed to copy this flower.'

The spires of a palace emerged out of a cluster of trees on the other side of the lake. In the distance, beyond the road and the buildings, miles and miles of sugarcane fields ended in low undulating hills. Kolhapur was known as the poor man's hill station. It was beautiful. I could only imagine what Dhondutai must have felt when she left all this behind for an unknown future in a grotesque big city. She had been about my age at the time. But far more innocent.

Two

There is another place of worship in Kolhapur, not too far from the Mahalaxmi temple. It is a temple of music. This was where Alladiya Khan once lived. Almost a hundred years ago, the king had gifted the building to his court musician. I had heard numerous stories about Khansahib and the days when he lived and practiced on the top floor.

It is a late summer evening. The Khansahib is on his way home after singing in the palace. That afternoon, in the king's private boudoir, he had rendered a strange composition about greedy kings taking over poor peasants' lands and leaving them to starve. Shahu Maharaj was first puzzled, then irritated, and finally he got the message. This was a tactic his beloved court musician had used before. If he wanted to convey something slightly unpalatable to the king, Alladiya Khan would sing it to him. This way, he caught the king in a good mood and also got his point across. People often approached the singer with their grievances and he would weave the issues into a composition. It always worked!

Alladiya Khan was deep in thought as he walked home that day from the palace. When they saw the tall, turbaned court musician in that mode, people on the street knew that he was probably composing some brilliant compound raga and would not disturb him with a greeting.

Those days, Alladiya Khan's close friend Bhalji Pendharkar, a film producer, was staying at his house. After a hearty dinner, Bhalji and young Bhurji Khan lay down, looking forward to being lulled to sleep by some sonorous, late-night raga from above.

They heard the sound of the tanpura. But to their surprise, for the next ten or fifteen minutes, only the drone of the tanpura wafted into the rooms. Its master's voice was nowhere to be heard. Bhalji got up and went upstairs to see what had happened to his friend. He saw the Khansahib sitting there, playing the tanpura as if in a trance, his eyes closed, a touch of a smile on his lips, like the Buddha.

The film producer went up close and peered into his friend's face. A few moments later, the Khansahib opened his eyes and said, 'Arre Bhaloo! What's the matter? What are you doing here?'

Bhalji Pendharkar stared at Alladiya Khan with a strange look. 'Err… Khansahib. We were just wondering… We heard only the tanpura for so long… We just wondered what had happened to you… '

Alladiya Khan laughed out loud. 'Oh! You see, today, when I sat down to strum the tanpura, its notes were in such perfect pitch and the sound so sublime, that I just couldn't bear to sing in the middle of it. I just wanted to listen to the sound of perfection.'

That afternoon, we saw the same tanpura encased in a faded mauve cloth case suspended horizontally from the ceiling alongside its longtime partner, whose head was turned the other way. They floated like encased mummies—long-dead, yet not discarded. They were hung so that they would not get in the way of the countless young feet that now crawled and skipped and walked around the house.

It was around four in the afternoon when we got to Alladiya Manzil. The building is located between a butcher shop and an optical store. A couple of children, their eyes thick with kohl, were playing with a tricycle on the street outside. Dhondutai nudged one of them and said, 'Where is your grandfather?'

'Inside,' the littlest one announced, matter-of-factly, hinting that Baba rarely moved out.

A man pulled up in a rattling two-wheeler. It was Baba's son, Nizam. 'Atya! How are you? Welcome! Please come in.' He touched her feet. I was thrown off. This couldn't be the same skinny teenager I had met almost twenty years ago when he came to learn music with Dhondutai! Baba had sent him to Bombay in the hope that at least someone from his family would keep the gharana going. However, he hadn't lasted very long because at some point, he needed to start earning a living and music was not going to give it to him.

When we entered the house, there was a sudden flurry of activity. Nizam said, 'Turn around. Turn around!' I was confused. Then I realized what was happening. Accompanying us that afternoon was Ninad, one of Dhondutai's students, who happened to be in Kolhapur visiting his sister. The directive was meant for him. His culpability? He was male. The women in Baba's family were not allowed to expose their faces to a male stranger. They had to throw on their veils before he could enter. Until they were suitably clad, he had to stand with his back to the door.

I was shocked. Such practices still exist in the twenty-first century? Dhondutai merely rolled her eyes and gave me a knowing smile, saying, 'I forgot all about that!'

Once the women had disappeared behind the cloth partitions hung up to separate the rooms, we entered. Baba was waiting inside with his big smile. 'Come, come!' he said. I touched his feet and was amazed at how little he had changed. One tooth from his front row was missing, but his glasses were the same opaque ones set inside a dark frame. His eyes twinkled a little less, but I attributed this to the darkness inside the house.

I looked around me, trying to catch a vestige of what this home must have once been like and a profusion of images played through my mind. There would have been the whiskered Alladiya Khan, his wife, and his three sons. Actually, two, since Badeji had moved at an early age to Uniyara, their hometown near Jaipur, after he fell ill. His brother Hyder Khan would have also been here. Perhaps they ate downstairs and slept upstairs. I knew the top floor was the music room. The tanpuras and tablas would have been lying around, alive and warm like human bodies.

But today there was none of that. The house had been divided, and further divided, to accommodate the growing family, and printed cotton sheets hung as partitions in the middle of rooms to create these spaces. We climbed up to the first floor, dodging two children who raced down the stairs.

'This one is Faeem's. That is Noor's. And these are Bhaiya's kids,' Baba said.

'How many of you live in this house now?' asked Dhondutai with a laugh.

'Seventeen!' replied Baba and laughed back, unabashed.

'Baap re.' Then her voice softened. 'So how have you been? Are you keeping good health?'

'All well, by the grace of Allah. Oh! Before I forget, there is a concert tonight at the Dewal Club. The secretary of the club wants to meet you.'

'Great! We will go! Oh, Baba, I must tell you about my encounter with you know who… ' Dhondutai said, and she launched into a long gossipy tale about her meeting with her long-standing rival and how, after years of bitterness and hatred, she had begun calling her regularly and telling her that she wanted to come and spend time with her. 'I know exactly what she wants from me, but she's not going to get it,' said Dhondutai firmly. She was referring to the rare ragas of this gharana, many of which had been taught to her by Baba himself.

'And Baba, you'd better not give out any of those ragas to any old person who comes to you either. You're always too generous.'

She confided in him, sought his advice, rebuked him for giving his secrets to her contemporaries. She talked and talked, telling him about all the things that had gone on in the last couple of years—how a particular concert had gone, or her ideas about a raga. It was like old times. Their friendship had lasted more than sixty years. In some ways, he was probably her closest friend.

A woman, her face fully covered with a veil, stood at the door holding a tray of biscuits and fried onion rings. She was waiting for someone to take them from her so she could go back behind the curtain and continue listening to the conversation from her secure spot.

Baba turned to me and said, 'You know how long we have known each other?'

'Yes, I have some idea,' I said, with a smile.

'Here. Try these. They were specially made because this recipe was given to my mother by my other mother, Ayi,' said Baba. 'They spent so much time together. Whenever my mother, was bored, or had had a quarrel with someone in the family, she would just walk out of the house and we all knew she had gone to the Kulkarni family. Sometimes she would stay for several days. She always came back with some delicious new vegetarian recipes. That is how close we were.'

I noticed that Dhondutai did not touch any of the food. She later told me that all her life she had hesitated to eat at a house where the utensils were used to make meats. This was something she could never quite get over. It was an unspoken understanding between the two families. They may have loved one another dearly, but certain cultural boundaries would never be crossed, and no one took it personally.

The phone rang, and one of the grandchildren ran up to Baba. It was for him, from the Dewal Club, the prestigious venue that had hosted the greatest musicians of India. One of the managers had heard that Dhondutai was in town, and wanted her, along with Baba, to be the guests of honour at a concert that evening.

The Dewal Club used to be an important hub in the history of Indian classical music. It was founded by a coterie of orthodox musicians and scholars who had the run of the place in the early part of the twentieth century. They prided themselves on their knowledge of ragas and music theory with an almost obnoxious ferocity, even if none of them could actually sing.

When senior musicians sang at the Dewal Club, they often started the concert with a teaser. They would set out the notes of a rare raga, and wait for one of these connoisseurs sitting in the front row to identify it. It was a challenge. In the process, the audience and performers kept one another on their toes.

Every few months, the Dewal Club music circle auditioned artistes to determine whether they were qualified to perform in their hallowed venue. A musician from Indore was once asked to audition before the club members. He sang a beautiful raga. When he finished and put down his tanpura, he found that instead of being attentive to him, his audience was deep in discussion about whether the third note should have been sharp or flat. The singer was so appalled with their response that he picked up his tanpura and walked out in a huff saying, 'I have no interest in singing before such a heartless audience, thank you very much.'

Evidently, audience tastes as well as performer standards at the Dewal Club had since plummetted, as we discovered that evening. The singer, a young woman from Calcutta, was unimaginative and repetitive. Dhondutai and I kept exchanging glances and secret smiles, childishly taking pleasure in the mediocrity.

Dhondutai and Baba sat on special chairs reserved for chief guests, under a line of portraits of all the greats in the music world. Baba had worn his fez that evening, for regardless of the music, he and his musical sister were back at the Dewal Club where once they had sat as children and heard the masters.

That night, after dinner, Dhondutai and I chatted about the day's events. We discussed how difficult it must be for Baba to live the way he was living. We joked about the singer from Calcutta at the Dewal Club, saying that if Kesarbai had been given the title 'Surshri' in Calcutta, we'd also better come up with an appropriate title for this singer. Within minutes, we were both fast asleep under enormous tents made of pale blue netting, designed to keep out the bugs. We had an important task to perform the next morning. We were going to sing at the goddess' temple.

Epilogue
Borivli

We were sitting in front of the little altar of gods in Dhondutai's flat in Borivli once again. Dhondutai's arthritic knees made it difficult for her to sit on the floor, so she now sat on a wooden stool and went through with the same ritual. It was raining and a gentle breeze carried in the scent of fried vermicelli. Dhondutai was wiping her gods clean with a soft white cloth, setting them down one by one. I sat next to her, rotating the sandalwood stick to make the yellow paste that would soon be dabbed on them.

By next week, they would all be gliding deep into the ocean, going back home. Dhondutai had decided to stay on in Bombay but she had also decided to set them free, just in case anything was to happen to her. That is, all but two. One was Ganesha, who she would continue to greet and bathe every morning. The other was a little laminated picture of the goddess. I had implored her to give it to me and promised that I would look after it forever.

I took the little picture and held her in my palm.

Last month, Dhondutai and I had both sung in the temple in Kolhapur. She had sat against the column that used to be stained with Alladiya Khansahib's hair oil and I had sat behind her and played the tanpura. The raga contained all our fears, our aspirations, our memories and our resolutions and we let the notes travel to the goddess' feet. I forgave my husband for whatever had come between us and decided in that moment that music would bind us forever. Dhondutai shut her eyes and let go of her anger towards the world.

We sang Sukhiya Bilawal, which I had learned specially for the occasion. As we unfolded the composition, several pilgrims came and touched Dhondutai's feet. Some lingered on, not quite sure why they were enchanted by the music. They wouldn't have known that these stone pillars had resonated with this offering of music a hundred years ago. Pushing through the crowd, a wizened old man wearing a white shirt, white pajamas, and a Gandhi cap came up to us and sat down, on his haunches, as if in a trance.

When we finished, we looked around, exhilarated. It was a feeling that no stage performance could replicate. The old man said, in a hoarse whisper, 'You are Dhondutai, right?'

She nodded. Her brow creased into a trishul and she tilted her head slightly while trying to recognize this person who knew her name.

'I am Oundhkar,' he said. 'I am eighty-six years old. I heard you sing when you were a little girl in this same spot, with Bhurji Khan guiding you, while your father accompanied you on the tabla. Your father and I also met several times in Narasimhawadi.'

'Arre wah!' she said. 'I think I may remember you. You lived in the grounds outside the palace and came to listen to us with your little child.'

'He was blind,' she added softly.

'Yes. I am alone now. I have come here every morning for the last eighty years. This is a very special day.'

Dhondutai smiled and nodded.

'I don't know if you have achieved name and fame, tai, but your music has definitely reached the gods.' He turned to me. 'And you, my daughter. You have the voice of Kesarbai sitting inside you. You will sing one day. A small piece of advice: learn to commit. Stick it out even when the going gets rough. It will make a difference to your music, your love, your life.'

I looked at him in wonder, and my eyes welled up. He chuckled softly and shuffled away. Suddenly, he turned around and looked at me.

'And another small point. Work on your sa. Think of the peacock when you hit the note. Sa resides in the cry of the peacock...'

Perhaps he was just a whimsical old man. But I now sing every day, and my sa is gradually improving, a few sesame seeds at a time.

Dhondutai is ensconced in Bombay, as healthy as when I first met her, twenty-five years ago. She continues to teach me twice a week, and we both joke about how I should keep a peacock feather under my pillow.

'But that doesn't mean you stop practicing, you know,' she told me. 'You have a long way to go before your music dances like the peacock and swoops down like an eagle. Just push yourself a little harder.' She picked up some ash that had dropped from the incense stick in front of the gods, and smeared it across my neck like a blessing.

I helped her get up from the stool that sat on the paisley-patterned rug in front of the altar. She suggested that we nap for a while, before sitting down to learn an evening raga.

Dhondutai lay on her side, with her hand under her head, and started to snore gently, almost right away. I shut my eyes, and opened them for just a brief moment, to see the portraits of the bushy Khansahibs smiling down at me. I shut them again and within minutes, I was running around the lake in Kolhapur in my denim shorts, with a young girl who wore flowers in her hair and laughed in perfect pitch.

Acknowledgements

I'd like to first thank my mother, Meera, for pushing her little girl into the world of music. And my father, Bhagwat, who taught me to find wonder in the little things.

I am deeply grateful to the following: Purvi Parikh and Arvind Parikh, for all the wonderful musical conversations. Ram Guha, for his incredible encouragement. Gita Mehta, for her thoughtful suggestions. Sonny Mehta for seeing the potential in this. Deepak Raja, for always believing in me. My publisher, Chiki Sarkar, for making work such fun. Also, my editor Rajni George and agent, Anna Ghosh. James Anderson, for pushing me to convert boredom into art. Rachana Shah, Vikramaditya Motwane and Ishika Mohan for their creative contributions. My dear friends who endlessly encouraged me—you know who you are. Finally, Pratish Motwane, for loving music as much, and Chaitanya, my little earth angel.

Book acknowledgements

There are a number of books I have drawn material from: Lewis Rowell's *Music and Musical Thought in Early India,* Janaki Bakhle's *Two Men and Music: Nationalism in the Making of an Indian Classical Tradition,* CS Lakshmi's *The Singer and the Song,* Dan Neuman's *The Life of Music in North India,* Maureen McCarthy Draper's *The Nature of Music,* Ashok Ranade's *Hindustani Music,* and Peter Manuel's essay 'Music, the Media, and Communal Relations in North India, Past and Present'.

A note on the author

Namita Devidayal was born in 1968 and graduated from Princeton University. *The Music Room*, winner of the Vodafone Crossroad Popular Book Award 2007 and named an *Outlook* book of 2007, is her first book. A journalist with *The Times of India*, she lives in Mumbai.